The Element
Education for Teachers

What makes some teachers more effective than others? Which pedagogies and practices are fads and which are backed with quality evidence? Which teaching strategies give teachers the biggest learning bang for their buck?

The authors have surveyed the research literature and carefully curated 50 elements of effective teaching—elements such as direct instruction, executive functions, metacognition, motivation, and scaffolding—to answer such questions and demystify the secrets of master teachers.

Designed specifically for clarity and ease of use, this book is perfect for both new and experienced educators. Each element uses a consistent architecture: a simple definition, concise overview of the research, practical Dos and Don'ts for the classroom, and a select quote to inspire reflection.

The Elements of Education for Teachers is an essential addition to any teacher's library and important reading for teachers' professional development.

Austin Volz is Senior Learner-Experience Designer on the "Tiger Works" Research and Development team at Avenues: The World School. A recipient of both a Fulbright scholarship and Foreign Language and Area Studies Fellowship, Austin holds a bachelor's from St. John's College and a master's from the Harvard Graduate School of Education.

Julia Higdon is Senior Research Scientist on the "Tiger Works" Research and Development team at Avenues: The World School. Julia began her career as a teacher and holds a doctorate in education research from the Harvard Graduate School of Education.

William Lidwell is Vice President of the "Tiger Works" Research and Development team at Avenues: The World School. He is the author of several books, including the best-selling *Universal Principles of Design*.

Also Available from
Routledge Eye on Education
(www.routledge.com/k-12)

The Elements of Education for Teachers

50 Research-Based Principles Every Educator Should Know

Austin Volz, Julia Higdon, and William Lidwell

Routledge
Taylor & Francis Group

NEW YORK AND LONDON

First published 2019
by Routledge
52 Vanderbilt Avenue, New York, NY 10017

and by Routledge
2 Park Square, Milton Park, Abingdon, Oxon, OX14 4RN

Routledge is an imprint of the Taylor & Francis Group, an informa business

Library of Congress Cataloging-in-Publication Data
Names: Volz, Austin, author. | Higdon, Julia, author. | Lidwell,
    William, author.
Title: The elements of education for teachers : 50 research-based
    principles every educator should know / Austin Volz, Julia Higdon,
    William Lidwell.
Description: New York, NY : Routledge, 2019. | Includes bibliographical
    references.
Identifiers: LCCN 2018058872 (print) | LCCN 2019006432 (ebook) |
    ISBN 9781315101002 (ebook) | ISBN 9781138294639 (hbk) |
    ISBN 9781138294653 (pbk) | ISBN 9781315101002 (ebk)
Subjects: LCSH: Effective teaching. | Instructional systems—Design. |
    Learning.
Classification: LCC LB1025.3 (ebook) | LCC LB1025.3 .V65 2019 (print) |
    DDC 371.102—dc23
LC record available at https://lccn.loc.gov/2018058872

ISBN: 978-1-138-29463-9 (hbk)
ISBN: 978-1-138-29465-3 (pbk)
ISBN: 978-1-315-10100-2 (ebk)

Typeset in Palatino
by Apex CoVantage, LLC

Dedicated to
Bill and Tamara Volz
Zac and Katrina Van Alst

Contents

Acknowledgments

The authors would like to thank numerous people who have made this work possible.

First, Connie Chen for that first tumultuous writing feedback to late-night parallel work sessions and all the meals, canceled plans, and pick-me-ups in between. Bill and Tamara for passing on the educator spirit and supporting a rampant consumption of books. Filip: So much sleep sacrificed between Lamont and Shanghai. Thank you for always encouraging a critical eye, good adventures, and pausing conversations to appreciate a well-crafted phrase.

We would also like to thank John Van Alst for his constant support and friendship during this project, as well as Jan Boyce, Al Boyce, and Pat Higdon for their abundant encouragement. And, of course, Jill Butler for her patient reviews, emotional support, and design wisdom.

Second, our colleagues at Avenues: The World School provided both direct and indirect support that helped bring this book into existence, especially Alison Mackey, Jeff Clark, Ty Tingley, Isil Çelimli, Charlie Xavier, Daniel Saniski, and all members of the "Tiger Works" R&D team.

Third, we would like to thank everyone at Routledge, especially Lauren Davis, for their patient commitment and professionalism in support of this work.

Introduction

We shape our tools, and then our tools shape us.

—John Culkin

Despite the great importance of education to families, industry, and society, we've not done particularly well giving teachers the tools for success. Much of education research remains in the confines of academia, hidden from teachers behind paywalls, dense tomes, or obscure, jargony language. The goal of this book is to bridge this gap with a concise, intentional translation of how to apply this research in practice.

Research, of course, changes. The criticism that schools still follow a factory model of education from 18th century Prussia is so common as to be nearly cliché. And yet, the need for change is not because centuries have passed, but because we now have a much deeper understanding of how students learn than in the 18th century. Psychology, sociology, economics, cognitive science, and numerous other disciplines have all contributed ways to promote students' learning. Similarly, in the coming decades, our understanding will continue to grow and change. Our current knowledge is likely imperfect, but teachers have to decide the best way to foster students' learning regardless of how imperfect the current state of knowledge. We provide teachers guidance to make good decisions grounded in the best available evidence.

The 50 elements in this book consist of laws, principles, guidelines, and proven heuristics. They were selected based on the strength of the research supporting them, their practical value to teaching, and their fundamental importance in the lives of teachers. Teaching is an exceptionally busy profession, yet much of the relevant writing is dense, the research quality varied, and the practical implications unclear. Thus, in this book, brevity and utility have been paramount. Arranged in alphabetical order, teachers can quickly reference each principle and within a few minutes take away valuable practices without having to wade through hundreds of pages of text.

Our goal is to provide teachers with a "heuristic toolbox" (see **Decision Making**) from which teachers can choose judiciously. This approach complements the meta-synthesis and meta-analysis approaches, popularized by John Hattie, Robert Marzano, and others. A meta-analysis combines the results from multiple studies so as to obtain an effect size: a standardized measure of a teaching strategy's effectiveness. While the resulting effect size offers a valuable way to compare and rank teaching strategies, it has its limits. First, a meta-analysis may include studies with teaching strategies that are poorly defined or difficult to implement. This variability results in a low overall effect size that can undervalue potentially powerful teaching strategies. Second, teaching strategies that are more highly ranked are not always preferable. Teaching is an art of selecting the right tool for the job, whether it be increasing engagement or enabling students to apply their knowledge in a range of contexts. Research cannot replace a teacher's judgment, but it can empower it.

Each element has a consistent two-page structure. The left-hand page provides the definition, an overview of the research, why the principle matters, and how it works. These paragraphs are followed by a "see also" section of related principles. The page ends with selected research for those who want to dive in more deeply. The right-hand page extracts guidelines are in the form of "DOs" and "DON'Ts" for applying the principle in practice. These guidelines are not exhaustive. Rather, they are meant to demonstrate concrete applications and prevent possible misinterpretations, sketching the boundaries for you to apply the element in other ways. While following the guidelines will increase the probability of successful learning, they are not absolute: context, logistical constraints, priorities, and other factors may influence what the right decision is. The element wraps up with a quote to inspire reflection.

The use of research-based elements in teaching puts excellent, effective teaching in reach. Use *The Elements of Education for Teachers* as a resource to increase your knowledge of education, as a tool for problem solving and brainstorming, and as a way to discover less frequently referenced education tools. Perhaps most importantly, use it to increase the effectiveness of your instructional practice, creating a research-based foundation to the art of teaching.

Austin Volz
Julia Higdon
William Lidwell

1 80/20 Rule

The majority of effects in any large system are caused by a few causes.

The 80/20 rule, also known as the Pareto principle, asserts that approximately 80 percent of the effects in large systems are caused by 20 percent of the variables in that system. The person who first recognized the ubiquity of the 80/20 distribution, the Italian economist Vilfredo Pareto, observed that 80 percent of the land in Italy was owned by 20 percent of the population. After some additional analysis, he realized this distribution described not only wealth in Italy, but in all countries—and astonishingly, in large, complex systems generally, including those in economics, management, quality control, and education, to name a few. He reputedly even discovered that 80 percent of the peas from his garden came from 20 percent of the peapods. A few examples of the 80/20 rule in education include the following:

- Twenty percent of school activities account for 80 percent of the academic results.
- Twenty percent of what is taught represents 80 percent of what is learned.
- Twenty percent of students require 80 percent of the time and resources.
- Twenty percent of learning outcomes underpin 80 percent of learning standards.
- Twenty percent of words in a language are used 80 percent of the time in conversation.

The specific percentages 80/20 are unimportant—it could be 70/30, 90/10, and so on. What is important is that a small number of variables drive the bulk of performance, and focusing on these high-leverage variables is the most efficient way to change a system. For example, 80/20 analysis has been used to identify the critical 20 percent of errors made by writing students. Using the results of this analysis, teachers were able to then target their instruction, practice, and grading on areas that produced the most improvement with the least effort. Similar 80/20 applications can be applied to enacting curriculum. Focusing instruction on a Pareto subset of a comprehensive curriculum runs contrary to coverage-driven approaches found in many schools today, but it will yield superior outcomes with less effort than exhaustive approaches.

Note that knowing what not to focus on is equally important. The time, energy, and money spent optimizing (i.e., improving system performance a small amount) are often as costly or costlier than that required to improve the critical 20 percent. Similarly, when redesigning processes and systems to increase efficiency (e.g., classroom activities, school schedules, professional development) focusing on aspects beyond the critical 20 percent yields diminishing returns. And not only do improvements beyond the critical 20 percent result in nominal gains, these gains are also often offset by the introduction of errors and new problems. In other words, efforts that can only achieve nominal gains come with risks that they can actually make things worse.

See also Decision Making; Errors; Intelligence; Performance Load; Personality

The seminal work on the 80/20 Rule is *Quality Control Handbook* by Joseph Juran (Ed.), 1951, McGraw-Hill; *The 80/20 Principle: The Secret to Achieving More With Less* by Richard Koch, 1999, Doubleday; "Applying the Pareto Principle to the Analysis of Students' Errors in Grammar, Mechanics and Style" by Kathryn O'Neill, *Research in Higher Education Journal*, May 2018, 34, 1–12.

DO

- Do use the 80/20 rule to assess the value of programs, target areas of redesign and improvement, and focus time and resources in an efficient manner.
- Do apply the 80/20 rule to admissions processes, curriculum design, lesson planning, learning activities, and examinations.
- Do formalize conferences and feedback to identify critical and noncritical content, skills, behaviors, and work.
- Do consider cutting or minimizing investment in noncritical elements that are part of the noncritical 80 percent.
- Do limit the application of the 80/20 rule to systems that are influenced by many small and unrelated effects.

DON'T

- Don't assume or treat all variables in a system as if they are equal.
- Don't optimize noncritical variables when time and resources are limited, or when the risk of setting performance back is unacceptable.
- Don't be discouraged by political resistance: getting organizations of all types to focus on the critical 20 percent is hard.

REFLECT

The 80/20 Principle can and should be used by every intelligent person in their daily life, by every organization, and by every social grouping and form of society. It can help individuals and groups achieve much more, with much less effort. The 80/20 Principle can raise personal effectiveness and happiness. It can multiply the profitability of corporations and the effectiveness of any organization. It even holds the key to raising the quality and quantity of public services while cutting their cost.

—Richard Koch

The 80/20 Principle: The Secret to Achieving More With Less by Richard Koch, 1999, Doubleday.

2 Ability Grouping

Grouping students for instruction according to abilities, aptitude, or achievement.

Ability grouping is the grouping of students by ability or attainment to optimize student achievement and simplify the planning and delivering of instruction. There are two basic types: within-class and between-class. Within-class ability grouping is forming small groups of students with similar abilities or attainment within a classroom. Between-class ability grouping is forming different classrooms of students with similar abilities or attainment.

Both forms of ability grouping are popular, but also perilous: popular because they make instruction more efficient for teachers, but perilous because this simplification comes at a price. Students grouped into low- or moderate-ability levels often internalize lowered expectations from teachers and peers, and this reduced self-concept can continue for years. Additionally, these students lose the opportunity to access higher-level content and learning processes and to learn from their higher-achieving peers. In extreme cases, ability grouping can lead to persistent student groupings (sometimes referred to as *streaming* or *tracking*), which creates strata in achievement and lifetime outcomes that are stark and often biased with regard to race, class, and gender.

Given these perils, the general rule should be to favor mixed-ability groups and adapt teaching practices accordingly. For example, teachers working with mixed-ability groups can make use of cooperative, peer-to-peer learning processes. Providing cooperative activities for a mixed-ability group enables students of higher abilities to recognize the gaps between their own abilities and those of students of lower abilities, observe instruction that reviews and consolidates content, and engage in peer-instruction. These learning processes deepen understanding, particularly when students are aware of these benefits. Students of low- and moderate-abilities also benefit from their higher-ability peers and gain exposure to students who may have higher levels of interest, investment, and enthusiasm for the content. With mixed-ability groups, there are two keys: accurate knowledge of students' abilities and a sufficient number of students of low-, moderate-, and high-abilities to evenly distribute across groups to prevent students from feeling isolated.

There is one exception to this general rule: students of very high ability—i.e., one year or more above grade level—benefit from between-class grouping to provide accelerated or enriched curricula. But these prodigies aside, the rule should be to mix and match.

See also   Classroom Management; Expectation Effects; Intelligence; Peer Tutoring

"What One Hundred Years of Research Says About the Effects of Ability Grouping and Acceleration on K–12 Students' Academic Achievement: Findings of Two Second-Order Meta-Analyses" by Saiying Steenbergen-Hu et al. *Review of Educational Research*, 2016, 86(4), 849–899; "Meta-Analytic Findings on Grouping Programs" by James Kulik and Chen-Lin Kulik, *Gifted Child Quarterly*, 1992, 36(2), 73–77.

DO ···

- ◆ Do generally favor mixed-ability groups both within and between classes.
- ◆ Do structure groups so that students work together and help each other.
- ◆ Do ensure that groups are temporary and appropriate for the unit of instruction.
- ◆ Do ensure that groups are constituted only for brief periods, one or two class meetings or the duration of one project.
- ◆ Do use formative and summative assessment evidence to accurately understand student ability and attainment.
- ◆ Do group high-ability students who are more than a grade level above their peers and have the interest to participate in accelerated or enriched classes.

 DON'T ··

- ◆ Don't generally form classes based on student ability.
- ◆ Don't establish rules that prevent students from switching between groups.
- ◆ Don't create long-term ability groups since it can result in tracking.
- ◆ Don't label groups of students by ability level.
- ◆ Don't form "advanced" versions of courses for students who are less than one grade level above their peers.
- ◆ Don't communicate low expectations in any groups.

REFLECT ···

Ability grouping rarely benefits overall achievement, but it can contribute to inequality of achievement, as students in high groups gain and low-group students fall farther behind. The more rigid the tracking system, the more likely these patterns are to emerge.

—Adam Gamoran

"Synthesis of Research: Is Ability Grouping Equitable?" by Adam Gamoran, *Educational Leadership*, October 1992, 50(2), 11–17.

3 Assessment, Formative

Gathering evidence of student growth during instruction to continuously tune teaching and learning activities and improve attainment.

Formative assessment engages teachers and students to answer three basic questions throughout the learning process: Where is the student trying to go? Where is the student now? How can the student close the gap? Answering these questions involves an iterative process of identifying and communicating the learning goals, collecting evidence that confirms progress toward those goals, adjusting or designing new instruction based on evidence, and repeating continuously until the goals are achieved.

The benefits of formative assessment are significant. Take a middle-ranked student from a class of 100 students. Give that student only one formative assessment during a 15-week period and research suggests that their class ranking would improve by about 14 students. A formative assessment every week will increase their ranking by about 25 students and twice a week by about 29 students. Generally, the more formative assessments the better. For students with lower class rankings, the gains would be greater.

Clearly communicating learning intentions and assessment criteria are critical success factors to any formative assessment strategy. Such practices focus teacher planning and facilitate student learning by clearly setting expectations about the learning experience. And research clearly supports the practice of explicitly communicating learning goals and assessment criteria to students. Not only do students who receive explicit goal and assessment information outperform students who do not but also the habits formed make them more efficient learners in future learning contexts.

But as with all forms of assessment, formative assessment takes time and resources, which can reduce instructional time and increase administrative burden. Here are some strategies to maximize the benefits and minimize the costs:

- Include both formal and informal formative assessments. Formal formative assessments include things like quizzes. Informal formative assessments include things like teacher observations of students during activities or ongoing work.
- Include formative assessment tasks that reflect the learning goals and are not separate from instruction.
- Keep formative assessments short. Short assessments, as opposed to lengthy classroom tests, lead to greater gains.
- Reduce grading and increase targeted feedback that helps students improve.

See also Assessment, Self; Assessment, Summative; Feedback

"Assessment and Classroom Learning" by Paul Black and Dylan Wiliam *Assessment in Education: Principles, Policy & Practice*, 1998, 5(1), 7–74; "Effects of Frequent Classroom Testing" by Robert Bangert-Drowns et al. *Journal of Educational Research*, 1991, 85(2), 89–99.

DO ···

- ◆ Do continually try to answer three questions: Where is the student trying to go? Where is the student now? How can the student close the gap?
- ◆ Do communicate learning goals and assessment criteria to students.
- ◆ Do use formative, summative, and self-assessments as evidence of student status relative to learning goals.
- ◆ Do leverage informal formative assessments to keep the administrative costs low.
- ◆ Do generate reports for formal formative assessments for students, teachers, parents, and school leaders with graphical representations of student data when possible.
- ◆ Do specify to students what they will need to do to reach their goals.
- ◆ Do use formative assessment to adjust instructional and learning design in an ongoing, iterative process.
- ◆ Do emphasize learning progress over grades.

DON'T ···

- ◆ Don't include learning goals beyond the current unit as part of formative assessments.
- ◆ Don't include learning goals in formative assessments that lack specific assessment criteria.
- ◆ Don't include behaviors such as effort or attendance in formative scores or grades.
- ◆ Don't give a formative assessment (such as a "pop quiz") as punishment.
- ◆ Don't provide non-specific feedback like "good" or "excellent."
- ◆ Don't overwhelm students with too much feedback.
- ◆ Don't generate reports for informal assessments.
- ◆ Don't report assessment results that promote student labeling or comparison.

REFLECT ···

There is a body of firm evidence that formative assessment is an essential component of classroom work and that its development can raise standards of achievement. We know of no other way of raising standards for which such a strong prima facie case can be made.

—Paul Black and Dylan Wiliam

"Inside the Black Box: Raising Standards Through Classroom Assessment" by Paul Black and Dylan Wiliam, *Phi Delta Kappan*, October 1998, 80(2), 139–148.

4   Assessment, Self

Assessment of oneself, by oneself, for oneself.

Self-assessment occurs when students evaluate their own performance or growth against specific goals and then identify strategies to achieve those goals. For example, students might predict how well they will do on an upcoming assessment, rate or grade their own work against a model or rubric, or reflect on their learning and devise ways to improve their understanding. Students who become practiced at self-assessment techniques like these evaluate themselves as well as teachers, outperform peers who do not self-assess, experience greater motivation in their learning, and develop essential self-regulation and metacognitive skills. For example, take a middle-ranked student from a class of 100 students where self-assessment isn't practiced. Teach this student to self-assess and give them a few weeks of practice, and research suggests their class ranking would improve by about 16 students. Lower-achieving students would improve their ranking by about 21 students.

However, in order for self-assessment to be productive, students need to achieve a prerequisite level of self-awareness and subject-matter understanding, making it a more effective strategy for older, experienced students versus younger, novice students. Students need to be able to understand objective criteria to the point that they can be accurate judges and critics of their own work, identify the gaps between their own performance and the desired performance, understand how to devise strategies to improve, and adjust their plans and behaviors accordingly. There are seven key factors that determine the efficacy of self-assessment:

1. Students are older and academically advanced.
2. Students are given clear goals and reference points against which to measure.
3. Students self-assess on tasks that are connected to recent teaching.
4. Students use structured rubrics to support their self-evaluation.
5. Students receive instruction on how to accurately self-assess.
6. Students compare their self-evaluations with teacher and peer evaluations.
7. Students feel safe engaging in honest reflection and self-critique.

Self-assessment has its pitfalls: biases, lack of motivation, the time required to train students, and, of course, concerns about grade inflation. These pitfalls can generally be mitigated by comparing and aligning self-ratings with teacher and peer assessments, training students about the different kinds of biases that compromise assessment accuracy, proactively educating parents about the benefits of the method, and maintaining a climate of high expectations and psychological safety.

See also   Assessment, Formative; Expectation Effects; Metacognition; Motivation

---

"Self-Grading and Peer-Grading for Formative and Summative Assessments in 3rd through 12th Grade Classrooms: A Meta-Analysis" by Carmen Sanchez et al., *Journal of Educational Psychology*, 2017, 109(8), 1049–1066; "Student Self-Assessment" by Gavin Brown and Lois Harris in J.H. McMillan (Ed.), *The SAGE Handbook of Research on Classroom Assessment*, 2013, Sage Publications, 367–393.

DO

- Do give students clear goals and reference points against which they can evaluate themselves.
- Do limit self-assessments to tasks connected to recent teaching.
- Do provide students structured rubrics to support their self-evaluation.
- Do instruct students on how to accurately self-assess before using it as an assessment technique.
- Do encourage students to compare their self-evaluations with teacher and peer evaluations.
- Do create a safe environment that promotes honest reflection and self-critique.
- Do educate parents and students about the benefits and potential pitfalls of self-assessment.

 **DON'T**

- Don't use student self-assessment with beginners or students who do not possess an accurate understanding of the criteria.
- Don't use self-assessments that are normative, where students compare themselves to other students in a scored or ranked system.
- Don't confuse self-assessment with self-grading—a teacher can have students self-assess their work without it resulting in a grade.
- Don't include student self-grades in report cards or transcripts.
- Don't use self-assessment as the only assessment technique—complement it with formative and summative assessments.

REFLECT

Student self-assessment can contribute to improved learning outcomes and better self-regulation skills, provided such self-evaluation involves deep engagement with the processes affiliated with self-regulation (i.e., goal setting, self-monitoring, and evaluation against valid, objective standards). It would appear that it is not the form of self-assessment per se but rather the level of mental engagement students must use to determine how well they have done.

—Gavin Brown and Lois Harris

"Student Self-Assessment" by Gavin Brown and Lois Harris, *SAGE Handbook of Research on Classroom Assessment* by James McMillan (Ed.), 2013, Sage Publications.

5 Assessment, Summative

Systematic measurement of student knowledge and skills at the end of a unit or course.

Summative assessments provide information about a student's final learning status at the end of a unit or course. Students can use this information as feedback to make adjustments to their approaches to learning to reach future goals. Teachers and school leaders can use this information as feedback to make adjustments to instructional and learning design to improve learning for future students. The goal of summative assessments is to evaluate and summarize student learning while maintaining student motivation, confidence, and desire to learn. Designing summative assessments that are both conclusive and authentic helps achieve this goal.

Summative assessments are conclusive when they include all of the most important learning goals and a sampling of the smaller goals, and the evidence regarding student standing relative to clear standards is unambiguous. For example, an assessment at the end of a unit or course should include tasks that require the demonstration of all of the most important learning goals. The feedback, whether it is in the form of a narrative or a score, should compare student performance against clear descriptions of what was expected. Summative assessment feedback should not include behavioral measures, such as effort and attendance. This feedback should be reported separately to avoid confusion with achievement. And norm-referenced reporting that compares students to each other can decrease motivation and should generally be avoided.

Summative assessments are authentic when students do a task that reflects a context outside of school, often in a demonstration or performance. For example, a road test to get a driver's license should include a live demonstration of driving in traffic. A knowledge test would not suffice. The authenticity of the task and its reflection of a real-world application of skills increase its usefulness as evidence of learning. Developing rubrics beforehand that include precise definitions of levels of performance and exemplars help ensure that the feedback accurately reflects student ability and is informative. When assessments include a practical demonstration, using the scoring rubric during the demonstration, rather than after, increases the accuracy of the feedback.

There are potential pitfalls with summative assessments, which can be demotivating to students and lead to decreased effort and learning, especially among lower ability students. Maintaining focus on increasing learning rather than on scores or grades, remaining non-judgmental, managing expectation effects, and keeping feedback private can help to mitigate these risks. All assessments should promote greater learning, and summative assessment is no exception. Providing a clear indication of student learning status at the end of a unit or course will help students and teachers understand their accomplishments and make adjustments to future instructional and learning strategies.

See also Assessment, Formative; Assessment, Self; Expectation Effects; Feedback

"Research on Classroom Summative Assessment" by Connie Moss, *SAGE Handbook of Research on Classroom Assessment* by James McMillan (Ed.), 2013, Sage Publications, 235–256.

DO ···

- ◆ Do link summative assessments to the overall goals of the instructional unit.
- ◆ Do use summative assessment to describe the final status of student learning relative to goals.
- ◆ Do include all of the most important learning goals in summative assessments.
- ◆ Do include a sample of lower-priority learning goals.
- ◆ Do use scoring guides and rubrics to evaluate demonstrations and performances.
- ◆ Do use authentic assessments as evidence of student performance in out-of-school contexts.
- ◆ Do favor assessment-reporting techniques that discourage students from comparing themselves (e.g., comments are preferable over grades).
- ◆ Do consider non-traditional summative assessments, such as exhibitions, performances, and portfolio reviews.
- ◆ Do provide students, fellow teachers, parents, and school leaders with the results of summative assessments.

DON'T ···

- ◆ Don't record performance assessment data after performances.
- ◆ Don't provide clues, hints, or suggestions during a summative assessment.
- ◆ Don't include behavioral measures, such as on-time completion, attendance, or participation in summative assessment scores.
- ◆ Don't distract from summative assessment results with unrelated extra-credit assignments.
- ◆ Don't use summative assessment results or grades to reward or punish students.
- ◆ Don't compare students to other students in summative assessment reporting, or by grading on a curve.

REFLECT ···

A genuine test of intellectual achievement doesn't merely check "standardized" work in a mechanical way. It reveals achievement on the essentials, even if they are not easily quantified. In other words, an authentic test not only reveals student achievement to the examiner, but also reveals to the test-taker the actual challenges and standards of the field.

—Grant Wiggins

"A True Test: Toward More Authentic and Equitable Assessment" by Grant Wiggins, *Phi Delta Kappan Magazine*, 2011, 92(7), 81–93.

6   Choice Overload

Having too many options can result in dissatisfaction and reduced performance.

When it comes to choice, you can have too much of a good thing. Giving students options that are too complex or too great in number can overload them, creating dissatisfaction and reducing performance. But too few options can be equally dissatisfying. For example, people given one or two choices tend to be as unhappy as people given 15 or more choices. So, the question is how much choice is the right amount? It's a complicated question because the potential benefits of more options come at the cost of increased cognitive loads associated with choosing from larger assortments—it is a tradeoff between preference and performance.

Generally, everyone prefers as much choice as possible—but what people prefer does not always correspond to that which brings about their best performance. For example, assume a set of choices about different ways to study a topic with no dominant option—i.e., all options are superficially equally attractive. When students are new to the topic, they are more likely to make poor choices and experience high post-choice regret. They benefit from minimal or no choice. When students are familiar with the topic, they are likely to make reasonably good choices and experience moderate post-choice regret. They benefit from three to five choices. When students have mastery of the topic, they can parse through a large array of options without experiencing significant post-choice regret. They benefit from many options. Managing choice overload is critical for both student satisfaction and performance. When students choose from options tailored to their abilities and prior knowledge levels, they are both more satisfied and learn more effectively than when presented with too many or too few choices.

But there are cases in which all people benefit from fewer options. Case in point: times of stress. When people are under stress—e.g., high-stakes testing or public performances—increasing the complexity or number of options decreases performance, especially for concentration-intensive activities like creativity and problem solving. This has implications for both time-based testing and extrinsic rewards, both of which increase anxiety levels and degrade performance on complex tasks. Therefore, less choice is definitely more in these contexts.

While it may be in vogue to let students make strategic choices about their learning, it is more likely to overload than empower them. The best learning results when choice overload is managed—i.e., modifying the complexity and number of choices—to student abilities and knowledge levels.

See also   Performance Load; Progressive Disclosure; Student-Directed Learning

"When Choice Is Demotivating: Can One Desire Too Much of a Good Thing?" by Sheena Iyengar and Mark Lepper, *Journal of Personality and Social Psychology*, 2000, 79(6), 995; "Choice Overload: A Conceptual Review and Meta-analysis" by Alexander Chernev et al., *Journal of Consumer Psychology*, 2015(2), 333–358.

✓ DO

- Do tune the complexity and number of options to students' abilities: lower ability, fewer or no options and higher ability, more options.
- Do offer more options when students have relevant prior experiences and preferences.
- Do simplify the presentation of options whenever possible.
- Do minimize the number of choices students have to make in a day.
- Do avoid unnecessary choice when students are under stress.
- Do avoid time-bounded tasks involving complex decision making or problem solving.

✗ DON'T

- Don't offer options to beginners in an area of study.
- Don't require students to choose from more than five options, unless they are advanced in the area of study.
- Don't offer extrinsic rewards for making correct choices on complex tasks— for example, paying money for good grades on tests.
- Don't ask students to make difficult choices under time-bounded or stressful conditions.
- Don't surrender to students' stated preferences for more options.

❝ REFLECT

When people have no choice, life is almost unbearable. . . . But as the number of choices keeps growing, negative aspects of having a multitude of options begin to appear . . . the negatives escalate until we become overloaded. At this point, choice no longer liberates, but debilitates. It might even be said to tyrannize.

—Barry Schwartz

The Paradox of Choice: Why More Is Less by Barry Schwartz, 2017, Ecco.

7 Chunking

Grouping units of information to make them easier to process and remember.

People's minds are limited as to how much new information they can hold and manipulate. These limitations are largely due to working memory, which is like a mental scratchpad where information is temporarily stored when problem solving, recalling lists, or comparing two proposals. The general human limit of working memory is 4 ± 1 chunks—i.e., people can hold four to five new things in mind when first introduced to them. If students are presented more information than this, their working memory is overloaded and their ability to learn compromised. There is no known way to increase working memory, but its limits can be hacked by reducing the quantity and complexity of chunks to be learned. The following five strategies are effective chunking strategies:

- Separating. Try to memorize the ten-digit number 7948094312. Since this number is unfamiliar, it represents ten chunks, which exceeds working memory limits. However, separate this long sequence into three smaller sequences that abide working memory limits, such as 794–809–4312, and it is far easier to memorize. This is the basis for the design of the modern phone number convention.
- Classifying. Try to memorize a 16-step procedure. If the procedure is unfamiliar, this will be difficult. However, group the steps into four categories—e.g., preparation, production, evaluation, and delivery—and the procedure is easier to learn.
- Connecting. Try to memorize the seven colors of the rainbow in the correct sequence: red, orange, yellow, green, blue, indigo, violet. If you are learning this sequence for the first time, it will be challenging because the number of colors exceeds working memory limits. However, memorize the name-like acronym ROY G BIV, and seven chunks can be stored effectively as one chunk.
- Images. It turns out that a picture is worth a thousand words—or at least a lot of chunks. Diagrams, charts, and time-lines are very efficient strategies to efficiently present complex information while consuming comparatively little working memory.
- Patterns. Try to memorize the ten-digit sequence 0, 1, 1, 2, 3, 5, 8,13, 21, 34. If the sequence is unfamiliar, it represents ten chunks, which exceeds working memory limits. However, once you know the pattern—i.e., each number is the sum of the two preceding numbers—the sequence can be easily recreated using a one-chunk rule.

It is worth noting that as students approach mastery, items become stored in long-term memory as increasingly elaborate chunks. This process both frees space in working memory to process new information and makes it easier to process information related to the chunks in memory. This suggests that the complexity of chunks can be increased in accordance with the subject-matter expertise of students.

See also   Mnemonic Devices; Performance Load; Serial Position Effects

"The Magical Number Seven, Plus or Minus Two: Some Limits on Our Capacity for Processing Information" by George Miller, *Psychological Review*, 1956, 63(2), 81–97; "The Magical Number Four in Short-Term Memory: A Reconsideration of Mental Storage Capacity" by Nelson Cowan, *Behavioral and Brain Sciences*, 2001, 24, 87–114.

✅ DO

- Do consider chunking in the presentation of any information that is to be committed to memory.
- Do chunk instruction starting at the highest level of course organization and working down (i.e., the number of units in a course, the number of lessons in a unit, etc.).
- Do limit the number of chunks at each level of instruction to five.
- Do favor chunking information in logical, relevant ways when possible.
- Do leverage how different media afford the chunking of information. For example, a book page is a logical group, a computer screen is a logical group, a presentation slide is a logical group, and so on.
- Do make ample use of diagrams, charts, and time-lines in content design.
- Do chunk information in consideration of existing knowledge, increasing the complexity of chunks as student expertise develops.

❌ DON'T

- Don't introduce more than five new chunks at a time.
- Don't make chunks too long or complex—keep them short and simple.
- Don't chunk information at the expense of a cohesive presentation of information.
- Don't chunk information that is to be used as a reference. For example, don't chunk a dictionary.

❝ REFLECT

Spotting patterns is about finding redundancy in the information. You can compress the information into a different, smaller, and more useful form by spotting parts that repeat in some way or other, and, ideally, capturing the repetitions in a rule. If we can successfully turn any group of data into a pattern or rule, then near-magical results ensue. First, we no longer need to remember that mountain of data—we simply need to recall one simple law. But the benefits don't just stretch to memory. We're also, crucially, able to predict all future instances of this data, and so control our environment more efficiently. The rule may even capture something about the mechanism of the data, allowing us to understand it in a more fundamental way.

—Daniel Bor

The Ravenous Brain: How the New Science of Consciousness Explains Our Insatiable Search for Meaning by Daniel Bor, 2012, Basic Books.

8 Classroom Design

The features and fixtures of learning spaces that support effective education.

The potential impact of classroom design on education is significant, accounting for 15–25 percent of the differences in learning progress over the course of a year. Interestingly, the impact of overall school architecture and design outside of the classroom—e.g., size and configuration of the school, routes through the school, quality of external spaces—has little to no impact on learning, which indicates where design and budgetary resources should be focused: the classroom. Research suggests three aspects of classroom design matter most: (1) naturalness, (2) individualization, and (3) stimulation.

Naturalness refers to the quality of lighting, acoustics, air quality, and links to nature. Lighting has the greatest overall impact on student progress. Natural light should be favored when possible, but sufficient quantity and quality of artificial lighting is also important. Full-spectrum bulbs can be used to enhance classrooms with poor natural light. Acoustic dampening and insulation should be sufficient to minimize in-class echo and out-of-class noise. Well-ventilated classrooms rooms are essential to minimize CO_2 buildup—a common but generally unrecognized problem that impairs cognitive function—especially in small classrooms. Links to nature can include scenic views of outdoor settings like parks, but plentiful in-class greenery can be substituted for interior rooms and urban contexts.

Individualization refers to the degree to which the design enables a sense of student ownership. A room layout that can be easily modified, personal display areas and adjustable furniture can give students the ability to fit the space to their needs. Adjustable chairs and desks that are ergonomically designed for the age of students strongly correlate with learning progress. Classrooms that can be adapted to support breakout spaces, meeting nooks, and learning zones of various types work best, as they present numerous opportunities for collaboration and active learning.

Complexity refers to the shape of the classroom, use of color, and the level of clutter and decoration. Generally, students in grades 6–12 benefit from larger rooms with simple shapes (i.e., squares), and younger students benefit from more complex room shapes with specialized activity zones. Making rooms subject-specific or optimized for specific types of learning promotes learning, especially for math instruction. Students learn better in sparse, uncluttered rooms, but rooms should not be sparse to the point of being boring. White walls with accent colors work best, using warm colors for physically active spaces (e.g., play and fitness) and cool colors for mentally active spaces (e.g., creativity and problem solving). The color red, in particular, should be minimized in spaces designated for tasks requiring intense concentration and testing.

See also Choice Overload; Executive Functions; Performance Load

"The Impact of Classroom Design on Pupils' Learning: Final Results of a Holistic, Multi-Level Analysis" by Peter Barrett et al., *Building and Environment*, 2015, 89, 118–133; "How Colors Affect You: What Science Reveals" by William Lidwell, *The Great Courses*, 2013.

✓ DO

- Do prioritize classroom design over the design of other school spaces.
- Do favor natural light, using full-spectrum bulbs for interior rooms and for locations with poor natural light.
- Do provide controllable lighting through independent switches and dimmers.
- Do mitigate noise and reverberation with acoustic barriers and insulation.
- Do check classrooms' air exchange rates and CO_2 levels to ensure proper ventilation.
- Do connect the classroom to nature—window views, in-class greenery, etc.
- Do advocate for students to have ergonomic and comfortable furniture appropriate for their ages.
- Do design spaces according to unique subject requirements, especially math.
- Do create opportunities for students to mark and own the space, using nameplates, dedicated display spaces, adjustable seating and desks, etc.
- Do favor neutral-colored walls with color accents.
- Do favor warm colors for physically active spaces and cool colors for mentally active spaces.
- Do provide spaces to display student work.

✗ DON'T

- Don't make classrooms look generic and sterile.
- Don't clutter learning environments with decorations and student work.
- Don't use the color red in spaces designated for problem solving, creativity, or testing.

❝ REFLECT

Most new school building construction in the United States and the United Kingdom today is still pouring "old wine into new bottles," replicating the 30-student, 900-square-foot classrooms that both support and often dictate teacher-directed whole-group instruction. These environments will not support student learning of 21st century skills and will be seen in the coming years as outmoded learning spaces requiring a building retrofit.

—Bob Pearlman

"Designing New Learning Environments to Support 21st Century Skills" by Bob Pearlman in *21st Century Skills: Rethinking How Students Learn*, Solution Tree Press, 2010.

9 Classroom Management

Class expectations, processes, and norms that guide student behavior and enable learning.

Without a well-managed classroom, learning cannot occur. Some analyses suggest that classroom management has a greater overall effect on student achievement than any other variable in schools. Effective classroom management does not need to be complicated. In fact, most classroom management programs have a positive impact on student outcomes, which indicates that adopting a classroom management program of some kind is better than having no program at all. However, the most effective programs share a set of key attributes and practices that account for the bulk of their effectiveness:

◆ Begin at the beginning. Classroom management programs are most effective when introduced the first moment of the first day of class and then practiced and reinforced for the first two weeks. It is important to establish norms of conduct early before bad social habits can take root.

◆ Target social-emotional development. Programs that emphasize the development of empathy and the cultivation of positive student-teacher relationships are most effective. And the positive effects can produce a virtuous cycle: better student-teacher relationships develop social and emotional skills at the individual level, which creates more positive collaborations, which creates positive peer relationships, which creates a more positive classroom atmosphere, which reinforces social and emotional skills at the individual level, and so on.

◆ Co-create policies with students. Programs that involve students in the creation of a simple set of expectations and consequences are more effective than those that are imposed by the teacher. Emphasis should not be on just rule making, but on the kind of classroom students want to be in. For elementary students, the list should be limited to three to four expectations and three to four levels of consequences so they are easy to follow and enforce. For older students, the limit should be about seven.

◆ Fair and consistent administration by the teacher over time. The best classroom management programs are also applied school-wide and across classes. In cases where there is ambiguity in violations, consider processes that involve students in the adjudication.

The ultimate goal is for students to become self-disciplined and not reliant on teachers or programs to maintain appropriate and productive conduct. Self-discipline is developed over the long term as students increasingly internalize the goals of the classroom and are intrinsically motivated to participate.

See also Motivation; Social-Emotional Learning; Student-Teacher Relationship

"A Meta-Analysis of the Effects of Classroom Management Strategies and Classroom Management Programs on Students' Academic, Behavioral, Emotional, and Motivational Outcomes" by Hanke Korpershoek et al., *Review of Educational Research*, 2016, 86(3), 643–680; "The Key to Classroom Management" by Robert Marzano and Jana Marzano, *Educational Leadership: Journal of the Department of Supervision and Curriculum Development*, 2003, N.E.A 61(1), 6–13.

DO ···

- ◆ Do adopt a formal classroom management program and be unwavering in its execution.
- ◆ Do introduce classroom management from the very beginning of school.
- ◆ Do remain "with-it," noticing all misbehaviors and responding quickly but proportionately.
- ◆ Do favor classroom management programs that target social-emotional development and emphasize student-teacher relationships.
- ◆ Do engage students to co-create classroom management policies and even participate in adjudicating disputes or gray areas.
- ◆ Do emphasize the necessity of rules to create a classroom that all students want to be in.
- ◆ Do keep rules short and simple.
- ◆ Do strive for a fair, consistent, and predictable administration of policies over time, ideally across classes and grades as a school-wide program.

 **DON'T** ··

- ◆ Don't accept or ignore misbehavior.
- ◆ Don't change or make *ad hoc* rules on the fly.
- ◆ Don't give more than one warning when expectations are not being met.
- ◆ Don't delay addressing severe disciplinary problems.
- ◆ Don't take misbehavior personally.
- ◆ Don't remove students from class except in extreme cases where safety is threatened.
- ◆ Don't make students reliant on rewards and punishments.

 REFLECT ··

Successful teachers took pains to explain both the rule itself and the reason behind it to the children. This was important in helping the children to see the need for the rule and therefore, to accept it . . . in contrast to this middle of the road system with good explanations and built-in flexibility, the less well organized and successful teachers tended to have either no rules at all (so that they were continually making *ad hoc* decisions that distracted them from teaching tasks), or else to have so many rules that the rules became overly specific and essentially meaningless.

—Jere Brophy and Carolyn Evertson

Learning From Teaching: A Developmental Perspective by Jere Brophy and Carolyn Evertson, 1976, Allyn & Bacon, 212, 59.

10   Creativity

The ability to generate novel expressions of thought and novel solutions to problems.

Like intelligence and personality, creativity is a psychological construct strongly associated with many positive life outcomes such as healthy long-term relationships, happiness and mental health, and overall inventiveness. But unlike intelligence and personality, creativity can be developed relatively easily. For example, take a middle-ranked student from a class of 100 students ranked by their creativity. Give that student four weeks of creativity training, and research suggests their class ranking would improve by about 24 students. Creativity training that emphasizes problem identification, idea generation and evaluation, and application in real-world contexts is the most effective.

Problem identification refers to correctly identifying and framing problems to be solved, as well as identifying the constraints and barriers that need to be navigated to get to a solution. For example, one problem identification method is known as the "five whys" technique. This technique helps identify root causes to problems by having people ask why a problem exists ("Why do students waste food?") and then take the answer ("Because they take too much.") and ask why that answer is the case ("Why do students take too much food?"), and so on repeated five times. Teaching problem identification through techniques like five whys is the most effective way to improve general creativity.

After problem identification, idea generation and evaluation are the next most effective techniques. Idea generation refers to generating a large number and variety of ideas, and idea evaluation refers to getting feedback on the quality of the ideas generated. For example, one idea generation technique is called the "paperclip method." This technique teaches students to combine existing ideas or objects into new ones, typically starting with creative uses for paper clips. Practicing idea generation using techniques like the paperclip method with feedback increases the number, variety, and quality of ideas generated over time. Note that practice in group-brainstorming contexts can be both detrimental to idea generation and the creative development of individual students, and therefore should generally be avoided.

Lastly, practicing creativity with real-world goals and constraints is more effective than exercises in pure imagination or free expression. For example, thought experiments involving real-world physics (e.g., chasing a beam of light to understand the physics of light) are more fruitful than unconstrained explorations (e.g., doodling shapes or playing random keys on a piano). Real-world goals and constraints both guide and scaffold creative development, as well as facilitate transfer to real-world contexts.

See also   Dual Coding; Feedback; Play; Productive Failure; Scaffolding; Transfer

"Teaching for Creativity" by E. Paul Torrance *Frontiers of Creativity Research: Beyond the Basics*, Bearly Limited, 1987, 189–215; "The Effectiveness of Creativity Training: A Quantitative Review" by Ginamarie Scott et al., *Creativity Research Journal*, 2004, 16(4), 361–388.

DO ···

- ◆ Do emphasize problem identification as part of creativity training.
- ◆ Do encourage students to come up with a minimum number of ideas.
- ◆ Do integrate creativity instruction into a variety of classes and contexts.
- ◆ Do encourage students to generate multiple, different ways to achieve goals, solve problems, and express ideas.
- ◆ Do favor embedding creativity practice in real-world contexts with real-world constraints.
- ◆ Do provide feedback on the quality of ideas after the idea generation process.
- ◆ Do teach students how to critique and evaluate creative ideas.

 DON'T ···

- ◆ Don't encourage unconstrained imagining or expression.
- ◆ Don't incentivize creative work with rewards.
- ◆ Don't rely on the creation of elaborate imagery or metaphors to develop creativity.
- ◆ Don't provide feedback when students are in the middle of idea generation.
- ◆ Don't practice creativity through group brainstorming.

REFLECT ···

We're all born with deep natural capacities for creativity and systems of mass education tend to suppress them . . . it is increasingly urgent to cultivate these capacities—for personal, economic and cultural reasons—and to rethink the dominant approaches to education to make sure that we do.

—Ken Robinson

"Do Schools Kill Creativity?" by Ken Robinson, *TED*, 2006.

11 Decision Making

Making educational decisions that best prepare students for future success.

Teachers make educational decisions that impact their students every day. A few of these decisions have the luxury of being evidence-based, but most are necessarily of the triage variety just to keep pace with the torrent of daily challenges. Given this, the question is how to increase the quality of teacher decision making while also recognizing the real-world constraints that they face? The short answer: make evidence-based decisions easier to make. The longer answer is detailed next with three approaches to evidence-based decision making for educators:

Heuristic Toolbox: A heuristic is a practical approach that trades slow and optimal solutions for fast and good-enough solutions. The heuristic approach is common outside of education, for example in fields such as design and medicine. In this approach, practitioners focus on identifying and acquiring a set of tried-and-true practices—a "heuristic toolbox"—and then focus on mastering these tools. Removing tools that don't work is as valuable as adding tools that do: out with the snake oil, in with the penicillin. The heuristic toolbox is a robust and practical way to elevate evidence-based practices. This book is offered as a heuristic toolbox for teachers and is itself the product of a heuristic approach: the application of the 80/20 rule to educational research.

Meta-analyses: The body of research literature that bears on education is vast, inaccessible, and often contradictory. This is why meta-analyses—a form of analysis that basically summarizes the net effects of a large corpus of research—are so attractive: hundreds of research articles go in and one tidy summation of results come out. When done well, meta-analyses can help us make sense of it all, but even when done well they typically rest on a large number of questionable assumptions. For example, how does one combine the results of research on project-based learning when it varies so widely in practice? The answer is not very well. Which is why meta-analyses are useful at evaluating well-defined and easily measured practices (e.g., retrieval practice) but less useful for practices that are not well defined or easily measured (e.g., inquiry).

Popular Books: Educators by their nature love to educate, and so the appeal of being first to share the latest educational research with colleagues is irresistible. But popular books that present such research have been particularly unkind to the field of education. Emotional Intelligence. Grit. Growth mindset. Learning styles. Multiple intelligences. The list goes on. Some merely repackage well-established findings and phenomena in new marketing guise, while others promote unfounded and misleading approaches. The results have largely been to distract educators and divert resources from things that do work so as to appear cutting edge, all at the expense of students.

See also   80/20 Rule; Errors; Flexibility Tradeoffs

See, for example, *Simple Heuristics That Make Us Smart* by Gerd Gigerenzer and Peter Todd, 1999, Oxford University Press.

✓ DO

- Do favor a heuristic approach to making evidence-based decisions.
- Do create a "heuristic toolbox" to focus personal- and professional-development efforts.
- Do be open-minded about data-driven decision making to inform teaching and management practices.
- Do conduct local research to answer basic questions. Field experiments need not be fancy: take two groups, try things with one group and not the other, compare results, and modify practice based on the results.

✗ DON'T

- Don't accept meta-analytic results as the last word in educational effectiveness.
- Don't be too quick to adopt new learning strategies presented in books by authors popularizing their own research.
- Don't let data-driven decision making compromise the learning experiences of students, create undue administrative burdens for teachers, or radically alter pedagogy for the purpose of easing data collection.

❝ REFLECT

The best heuristics are those that encapsulate useful information in a way that is intuitive to remember and act upon but that are also specific to their context. Their power lies in their ability to induce people to take better actions. By carefully testing and vetting heuristics, we have an opportunity to create better ways to get knowledge and skills to those who need them, but which are designed to ensure that they are not misleading (as some that have developed over time can be), and that they encapsulate reliable science.

This process has the chance to transform the decision capabilities of individuals without needing them to devote significant chunks of their lives to acquiring in-depth knowledge of complex phenomena—but rather by giving them ways to act in ways that serve them well.

—Antoinette Schoar and Saugato Datta

"The Power of Heuristics" by Antoinette Schoar and Saugato Datta, *Ideas42*, January 2014.

12 Deliberate Practice

Structured activities that target the improvement of a specific skill.

Practice does not make perfect; perfect practice makes perfect. And what is "perfect practice"? The closest thing we know is a specific form of practice known as deliberate practice. Any skill can be mastered with sufficient deliberate practice, whether one aspires to become an expert chess or violin player, a professional basketball player or mathematician, or to enhance cognitive skills like creativity and critical thinking.

Three things distinguish deliberate practice from common conceptions of practice: (1) emphasis on component skills versus whole skills, (2) immediate and specific feedback versus delayed and general feedback, and (3) progressive difficulty that stays at the edge of student ability versus a fixed difficulty that involves mere repetition. These differences may seem subtle, but they make all of the difference.

Emphasis on component skills refers to focusing on the skills that comprise an ability: the footing, hip position, and proper force required to shoot a basketball, or the word choice, transitions, and complex sentence structure used in writing. The optimal way to improve a complex skill is to master its component skills in a systematic way, from foundational skills to tuning technique. This focused practice allows component skills to become increasingly automatic so that they can build on one another toward mastery.

Immediate and specific feedback refers to measuring performance, monitoring progress, and determining which kinds of practice activities are most effective. Feedback should be targeted and given immediately and allow students to incorporate the feedback into practice right away.

Progressive difficulty refers to adapting practice based on student performance to keep it challenging. As students master one component skill and move on to the next one, their practice should never be easy. A continuously difficult activity is typically not inherently motivating. This requires teachers, like coaches, to continually raise the bar while also motivating students.

Mastery can only be obtained through regular, high-quality practice over a significant period of time. Some estimates set the amount of practice needed to achieve mastery at 10,000 hours, popularly referred to as the "10,000-hour rule." However, it's quality, not quantity that counts. It is true that mastery requires a lot of deliberate practice, but no magic number exists. The requisite amount of time depends on the skill, person, environment, and quality of practice.

See also   Feedback; Interleaving; Motivation; Retrieval Practice; Scaffolding; Spacing

"The Role of Deliberate Practice in the Acquisition of Expert Performance" by Anders Ericsson et al., *Psychological Review*, 1993, 100(3), 363–406.

DO ··

- ◆ Do give students clear practice goals at the edge of their abilities.
- ◆ Do break practice into component skills that can be sequentially mastered.
- ◆ Do provide corrective feedback during practice, enabling students to practice needed adjustments.
- ◆ Do assign deliberate practice at least every other day for targeted skills, limiting practice sessions to 30-minute blocks with breaks as needed.
- ◆ Do ensure that practice sessions are continuously challenging and effortful: no pain, no gain.

 DON'T ··

- ◆ Don't blindly chase 10,000 hours.
- ◆ Don't provide students general or unactionable feedback—e.g., "try harder" is not good feedback.
- ◆ Don't provide untargeted "kitchen-sink" feedback.
- ◆ Don't assign practice that can be mindlessly performed.
- ◆ Don't assign practice that depends on unmastered component skills.

 REFLECT ···

Because deliberate practice was developed specifically to help people become among the best in the world at what they do and not merely to become "good enough," it is the most powerful approach to learning that has yet been discovered.

—K. Anders Ericsson

Peak: Secrets From the New Science of Expertise by Anders Ericsson and Robert Pool, 2017, First Mariner Books.

13 Depth of Processing
Engaging students to think hard about content to improve retention.

Memory doesn't just happen. It is a function of how hard and how long a student thinks and grapples with subject matter. For example, take two groups of students tasked to memorize word lists. The first is instructed to explain the emotions that each word evokes and the second to count the number of vowels in each word. When tested afterward, the first group will remember almost twice as many words as the second.

How deeply a student processes material is determined by how much the information is elaborated, its uniqueness, its relevance, and the frequency and modes presented. Students can elaborate content by connecting, explaining, or expanding upon it. Unique information attracts students' attention by standing out, whether by visually striking, presented in isolation, or by being surprising. Relevant information connects to students' prior knowledge and experiences. Presenting information repetitively in multiple ways (text, images, verbal, etc.) compels attention and mental processing.

And note that it is the mental processing of content, not mere participation in related activities, that creates the learning gains. Again, take two groups of students. The first group makes a diorama of a scene from a novel and the second group rewrites the scene to demonstrate different character traits. The first group will remember a lot about the process of designing and making a diorama—the materials, colors, layout, etc., whereas the second group will remember how the scene's structure and word choice developed the novel's characters. What students will remember is a function of what they spent the bulk of their time thinking about.

This has implications for critical thinking, as well as the countering of "fake news" and propaganda: incorrect information, when emphasized and repeated, is better remembered for the same basic reasons. For example, when students spend a long time developing erroneous theories or solutions and only receive brief corrective feedback, they will remember the incorrect information better than the correction because the erroneous was more deeply processed. Similarly, the mere act of highlighting what is not true, either by emphasizing its incorrectness or crossing it out in an essay, can make it more memorable than what is true.

Deep processing takes mental energy and cannot be sustained indefinitely. The deepest engagements should be prioritized for the most important learning, and work requiring intense periods of concentration should be interspersed with frequent breaks.

See also Mnemonic Devices; Retrieval Practice; Serial Position Effects; Spacing

---

"Levels of Processing: A Framework for Memory Research" by Fergus Craik and Robert Lockhart, *Journal of Verbal Learning and Verbal Behavior*, 1972, 11(6), 671–684. For a popular treatment, see "Students Remember What They Think About" by Daniel Willingham, *American Educator*, 2003, 27(2), 37–41.

✅ DO

- Do design assignments that focus attention and concentration on things related to important learning outcomes, not on tangentially related activities.
- Do have students relate their learning to familiar topics and experiences to increase their depth of processing.
- Do present information and engage students in multiple modes such as text, verbal, and images.
- Do highlight the most important information to make it stand out.
- Do match students' activities to the ways learning will be applied or recalled.
- Do try to avoid activities and assignments that can turn to thoughtless repetition.
- Do design assessments based on the relationships between material, not just the facts.

❌ DON'T

- Don't allow students to spend more time engaging with potentially incorrect things than with correct ones.
- Don't increase student activity for its own sake, especially when unrelated to learning outcomes.
- Don't design assessments with less depth of processing than was in the learning process.
- Don't provide brief feedback when students have spent significant energy on developing an incorrect answer.

❝ REFLECT

One of the interesting features of your memory system is that you don't control what is stored. Wanting to remember something doesn't have much bearing on whether or not you will actually remember it. Thus, the first principle for students is that memories are formed as the residue of thought. You remember what you think about, but not every fleeting thought—only those matters to which you really devote some attention.

—Daniel Willingham

"Ask the Cognitive Scientist: What Will Improve a Student's Memory?" by Daniel Willingham, *American Educator*, Winter 2008–2009, 17–25.

14   Direct Instruction

Explicit teaching using lectures or demonstrations of the material to students.

In direct instruction, a teacher, typically using a curriculum, decides what students work on and teaches them the information and skills they need to understand concepts and perform tasks. In contrast, in student-directed instruction students set their own goals or discover learning resources on their own. With few exceptions, direct instruction is one of the most reliable, scalable, and effective methods of instruction.

Direct instruction is often mischaracterized as inherently boring, creatively limiting due to prescriptive curricula and scripted lessons, and derided as the "banking method of education" (where teachers deposit their knowledge into students' minds). But teaching that is not creative, engaging, motivating, or active is simply bad instruction, not direct instruction. In fact, direct instruction where teachers exhibit enthusiasm, make content and curriculum relevant to students, and enable students to overcome difficulties is more likely to motivate students than leaving them to explore topics on their own.

Direct instruction is effective because (1) teachers are able to use their expertise to design learning experiences that emphasize essential concepts and skills, and (2) teachers are able to modulate the rate of new information to adjust performance loads. By teaching students important concepts and skills and providing relevant practice, students are able to learn more deeply. Alternatively, when students learn on their own, they often spend valuable time on inessential information and become lost or overwhelmed. Accordingly, good direct instruction limits the amount of new information taught to students through techniques such as interspersing practice activities, introducing skills through worked solution examples, and chunking related information.

There are three circumstances when it's preferable not to use direct instruction: (1) when students have advanced knowledge or general ability, (2) when the skills being learned have multiple correct approaches or complex conceptual elements (such as the calculation of standard deviation in statistics), or (3) when a skill has many complex, related elements and so is unlikely to be successfully taught in advance and remembered. For example, rather than abstractly teaching a child how to ride a bike, it is more productive to first allow them to try and then provide feedback and guidance. Students, of course, need to learn to become independent learners—to navigate complex problems, evaluate evidence and sources of information, and weigh competing viewpoints without teacher support—but these are best accomplished through direct instruction, not making students figure it out on their own.

See also   Chunking; Engagement, Student; Performance Load; Student-Directed Learning

---

"The Effectiveness of Direct Instruction Curricula: A Meta-Analysis of a Half Century of Research" by Jean Stockard et al., *Review of Educational Research*, August, 2018, 88(4), 479–507; "Why Minimal Guidance During Instruction Does Not Work: An Analysis of the Failure of Constructivist, Discovery, Problem-Based, Experiential, and Inquiry-Based Teaching" by Paul Kirschner et al., *Educational Psychologist*, 2006, 41(2), 75–86.

DO ···

- ◆ Do favor direct instruction for teaching large classes and for when the stakes of not learning are high.
- ◆ Do leverage existing well-designed, well-tested, well-sequenced teaching resources and materials.
- ◆ Do use techniques such as worked examples and chunking to minimize performance loads related with new material.
- ◆ Do adapt the quantity and rate of instruction to student abilities.
- ◆ Do use direct instruction to teach students to be independent learners and not dependent on the teacher.

 **DON'T** ···

- ◆ Don't let beginner students choose what to practice or what to learn.
- ◆ Don't use direct instruction for complex skills that are better experienced in applied versus theoretical contexts.
- ◆ Don't limit the application of direct instruction to rudimentary academic skills.
- ◆ Don't believe mischaracterizations about direct instruction: Skilled teachers can create learning experiences that are creative, engaging, and inspiring with direct instruction.

REFLECT ···

Project Follow Through was the largest and most expensive experiment ever conducted in the field of education. The experiment was funded by the U.S. federal government and designed to determine the most successful academic program for teaching at-risk children. The Direct Instruction model and over twenty other instructional models were systematically implemented in schools across the country in urban and rural settings. Thousands of students from very diverse backgrounds were administered the Direct Instruction programs. The results of Project Follow Through were clear-cut. Students taught with Direct Instruction had stronger academic growth and stronger self-concepts at the end of the intervention. No other curriculum produced these changes. Thus, the results demonstrated the success of the Direct Instruction model. They showed its success with at-risk students, as well as more affluent peers. Both groups experienced accelerated growth and success in comparison to students in other programs.

—Siegfried Engelmann

Engelmann's Direct Instruction: Selected Writings From the Past Half Century by Timothy Wood (Ed.), 2014, NIFDI Press.

15 Discussion-Based Learning

Teacher-facilitated conversations between students to develop understanding.

Discussion-based learning involves students in deliberate conversations facilitated by the teacher to deepen student learning. For example, a teacher may facilitate a discussion about classroom expectations so students better understand their purpose and internalize them. In a history class, a debate between opposing sides in a conflict helps students understand multiple perspectives. In a math class, students may discuss solutions to a problem in order to clarify logical steps in a mathematical proof. Discussion-based pedagogies have a long and storied history, especially in philosophy, but it has emerged recently as a strategy to engage marginalized learners, such as involving minority students in civic practices or girls in math and science.

This practice is gaining in popularity, but are students learning? Sometimes. Done well, discussion-based learning can foster deep learning and develop essential communication skills. Done poorly, it can devolve into unproductive chitchat. The five keys to successful discussion-based learning are (1) facilitating in-depth discussions with questions that address key learning objectives, (2) promoting an open exchange of ideas that engages all participants, (3) enforcing rules and norms of conduct around discussions, (4) having collegial relationships among the participants, and (5) acting as a facilitator and generally not participating in the discussions. The research suggests discussions are particularly effective at promoting reading comprehension, problem-solving, and critical thinking skills. The following are guidelines to consider in these contexts:

- Reading comprehension: Using discussion of texts to find, understand, analyze, and critique information presented promotes reading comprehension. This is true for students of all reading levels, and it is especially effective for students who read at lower levels. When discussion focuses on a text, it should include careful reading, connections to evidence, and demonstrations of background knowledge.
- Problem solving: Using discussion to solve problems is effective to identify and correct errors in thinking, guide the use of effective strategies, and develop skills in argumentation, particularly in math. This strategy is also referred to as collaborative problem-based learning. When discussion focuses on problem solving or proofs, it should reinforce clear logical steps and reasoning.
- Critical thinking and reasoning: The discussion of policies, controversies, and dilemmas is effective in the development knowledge, philosophical reasoning, argumentation, and pro-social attitudes. When discussion focuses on ideas, it should include careful examination of evidence, reference multiple perspectives, and prioritize rational deliberation over purely emotional responses.

See also   Engagement, Student; Feedback; Peer Tutoring; Teach-to-Learn

"Examining the Effects of Classroom Discussion on Students' Comprehension of Text: A Meta-Analysis" by Karen Murphy et al., *Journal of Educational Psychology*, 2009, 101(3), 740–764; "Discussion-Based Approaches to Developing Understanding: Classroom Instruction and Student Performance in Middle and High School English" by Arthur Applebee et al., *AERJ*, 2003, 40(3), 685–730.

DO

- Do align the focus of discussion with targeted learning goals.
- Do facilitate discussion so that it remains focused and purposeful.
- Do focus on the careful reading of text, consideration of evidence, and multiple perspectives, when applicable.
- Do highlight clear logical steps and reasoning, when applicable.
- Do reference relevant background knowledge and support student connections to background knowledge.
- Do use questions to guide discussion and to identify and correct errors.
- Do encourage students to respond directly to other students and to pose questions.
- Do support student responsibility for speaking, listening, responding, and staying on topic.
- Do cultivate a climate of trust and positive relationships to facilitate open discussion.
- Do favor discussion-based learning to support reading comprehension, problem solving, and critical thinking and reasoning.
- Do create rules of conduct and establish class norms to support safe and productive participation in discussion.

❌ DON'T

- Don't allow discussions to wander off topic or become non-purposeful.
- Don't respond to what every student says.
- Don't relax high expectations during discussions.
- Don't dominate classroom discussion or allow one or a few students to dominate.
- Don't rely on discussion alone to develop student understanding.

REFLECT

Discussion-based learning asks the students to discover the answer themselves. The teacher doesn't lecture or give the answer; the teacher leads the discussion by asking revealing questions. Great discussion-based teachers ask great questions.

—Tyler Tingley

Former head of school of Phillips Exeter Academy and Avenues: The World School. Quote shared in correspondence with authors, December 2, 2018.

16 Dual Coding

Combining verbal and visual cues to increase learning and retention.

People process and store information in what seems like a singular, unified process. However, the brain actually processes and stores verbal and visual information using two distinct cognitive systems, which interact to store and retrieve information in memory. Because these systems are independent, more information can be processed without cognitive overload using both systems together than either system alone. Or, stated simply, students learn better with words and images together.

Concrete words (like pendulum) are learned more readily and accurately than abstract words (like justice), because concrete words evoke imagery as well as conceptual information, demonstrating dual coding at work. The same is true for concrete versus abstract concepts. Students learn more when they are presented with information in both text and images, such as in multimedia or animation with narration, and when they are prompted to visualize new information or to comprehend text by constructing pictures or diagrams. For example, students who heard 20 novel statements after being prompted to visualize them learned about twice as much as those who were prompted to mentally pronounce them. This relates to a phenomenon known as the *picture superiority effect*: Information learned as images, real or imagined, is better retained than information learned as words. The reason, in dual-coding parlance, is that images are coded twice in memory and words just once—i.e., an image generates both a visual and a verbal code in memory, whereas words generate just a verbal code. So, true to adage, a picture does indeed paint a thousand words.

Four guidelines should be considered in the application of dual coding: (1) distribute information between verbal and non-verbal processes, (2) reduce unnecessary processing, (3) avoid redundancy, and (4) favor graphical displays for complex information. For example, it is helpful to use audio narration alongside an image instead of requiring students to hold the image in working memory while reading text. To avoid redundancy, do not include audio narration of written text, unnecessary pictures, or music. Lastly, when complex, multivariate data can be presented visually (e.g., in the manner of Charles Minard's classic infographics), they will be more deeply understood and better remembered than equivalent verbal representations.

Dual coding should not be confused with learning styles or types. All learners benefit from verbal and non-verbal information presented together. Students do have learning preferences and may gravitate toward particular modes of instruction, but they all learn better with both verbal and non-verbal information. Accordingly, it is not necessary or beneficial to match instruction to these preferences.

See also   Direct Instruction; Performance Load; Serial Position Effects; Study Tactics

"A Test of Two Alternative Cognitive Processing Models: Learning Styles and Dual Coding" by Joshua Cuevas and Bryan Dawson, *Theory and Research in Education*, 2018, 16(1), 40–64; "Dual Coding Theory and Education" by James Clark and Allan Paivio, *Educational Psychology Review*, 1991, 3(3), 149–210.

DO ···

- ◆ Do provide information in combined verbal and non-verbal forms when the learning outcome is complex.
- ◆ Do use mental imagery to help students understand abstract or complex concepts or phenomena.
- ◆ Do encourage students to process verbal information by drawing pictures, maps, graphs, or diagrams.
- ◆ Do teach students to make their mental imagery vivid and concrete.
- ◆ Do provide pictures, graphs, and diagrams alongside key verbal descriptions or text.
- ◆ Do allow more time for processing when information includes both verbal and non-verbal presentation.
- ◆ Do favor audio narration over written text when presenting alongside images.
- ◆ Do use multivariate charts, diagrams, and infographics to give learners a memorable "big picture" understanding of complex data.

 DON'T ···

- ◆ Don't present only verbal or non-verbal information when it is important that students remember it, or when the concept is difficult or complex.
- ◆ Don't repeat an exclusively verbal or non-verbal approach when students are struggling to grasp a concept.
- ◆ Don't include non-essential additional information, such as adding music to a presentation when the music is unrelated.
- ◆ Don't classify students as verbal or non-verbal learners and don't adapt instruction based on "learning styles."

 REFLECT ···

The research demonstrating that imagery and concreteness play central roles in the representation and acquisition of knowledge is directly relevant to instructional practices. The positive effects of concreteness and imagery on the readability of texts and on memory, for example, generalize to oral transmission of information in the classroom. That is, lessons containing concrete information and evoking vivid images will be easier to comprehend and remember than lessons that are abstract and not image-arousing. Moreover, the same imagery manipulations that benefit memory for text should also benefit memory for orally presented information as in classroom lessons.

—James Clark and Allan Paivio

"Dual Coding Theory and Education" by James Clark and Allan Paivio, *Educational Psychology Review*, 1991, 3(3), 173.

17 Engagement, Parent

Involvement of parents in and out of school to improve student learning.

Parents are their child's first teacher. Parents shape their children's beliefs, expectations, enjoyment, and investment in learning, and can have a significant impact on achievement. While there are different cultural norms concerning how parents and teachers interact, there is no question parental involvement is associated with increased learning among students of all cultural and economic groups and should be welcomed and invited. Students who have parents who are involved in their education achieve at substantially higher levels. For example, take a middle-ranked student from a class of 100 students where parents are not involved. If a parent gets involved in their learning, research suggests their class ranking would improve by about 19 students.

Setting high expectations, having a supportive parenting style, and tutoring at home are the most effective forms of involvement. For example, parents who listen to their children read and actively teach their children can successfully improve their children's abilities. However, not all forms of parent involvement are helpful. For example, attending school events is more strongly linked with positive teacher perceptions than students' academic achievement. And excessive home supervision, such as overmonitoring screen time and micromanaging homework, can be harmful.

Three techniques for engaging parents have demonstrated particular effectiveness:

1. Teacher Invitations: Parents are more likely to be involved and are more motivated when they receive specific invitations from teachers.
2. Informative Parent-Teacher Conferences: Parents need clear information about how their child is doing relative to their learning goals. Providing parents with accurate and specific information about their child's achievement and academic needs increases credibility and trust.
3. Parental Support Coaching: Providing support for parents who are willing and able to tutor their children at home. For example, coaching parents to maintain high expectations, employing a supportive versus surveillance style of parenting, and avoiding micromanaging or helping children with their homework.

While there is evidence that voluntary parent involvement is beneficial, school programs designed to increase parent involvement lack evidence of success. To raise student achievement, it is better to focus on other strategies with stronger evidence. For example, rather than institute a parent-involvement program at school, it is better to nurture natural parental involvement and build relationships with parents in the classroom.

See also Engagement, Student; Homework; Sleep Strategies; Social-Emotional Learning

"Effects of Parental Involvement on Academic Achievement: A Meta-synthesis" by S. Wilder, *Educational Review*, 2014, 66(3), 377–397. For a popular treatment, see *Powerful Partnerships: A Teacher's Guide to Engaging Families for Student Success* by Karen Mapp et al., 2017, Scholastic Press.

DO ⋯⋯⋯⋯⋯⋯⋯⋯⋯⋯⋯⋯⋯⋯⋯⋯⋯⋯⋯⋯⋯⋯⋯⋯⋯⋯⋯⋯

- ◆ Do treat parents as partners versus adversaries.
- ◆ Do encourage parents to maintain high expectations and goals for their children.
- ◆ Do provide parents with accurate, clear, and specific information about their children's achievement and needs.
- ◆ Do provide resources and training for parents who are willing and able to tutor their children.
- ◆ Do try to understand parent perspectives, challenges, and beliefs about education and the parental role.
- ◆ Do proactively build relationships with parents.

 DON'T ⋯⋯⋯⋯⋯⋯⋯⋯⋯⋯⋯⋯⋯⋯⋯⋯⋯⋯⋯⋯⋯⋯⋯⋯⋯⋯

- ◆ Don't encourage parents to monitor their children's homework.
- ◆ Don't tell parents they should lower expectations and aspirations for their children.
- ◆ Don't discourage parents who want to be involved.
- ◆ Don't spend resources instituting parent-involvement programs.
- ◆ Don't interpret the lack of parent participation in events or other initiatives as lack of caring about their child's education.

REFLECT ⋯⋯⋯⋯⋯⋯⋯⋯⋯⋯⋯⋯⋯⋯⋯⋯⋯⋯⋯⋯⋯⋯⋯⋯⋯⋯⋯⋯⋯⋯

The way schools care about children is reflected in the way schools care about the children's families. If educators view children simply as students, they are likely to see the family as separate from the school. That is, the family is expected to do its job and leave the education of children to the schools. If educators view students as children, they are likely to see both the family and the community as partners with the school in children's education and development.

—Joyce Epstein

"School, Family, and Community Partnerships: Caring for the Children We Share" by Joyce Epstein, *School, Family, and Community Partnerships: Your Handbook for Action*, 2002, Corwin Press, 7–29.

18 Engagement, Student
The level of student attention, interest, and emotional investment during instruction.

Engaged students learn more and perform better on standardized tests. They have lower dropout rates, achieve higher levels of academic success, and are more likely to persist through academic struggles. Indications of engaged students (sometimes referred to as "look-fors") include the following:

- Active participation in the learning activities, such as quickly beginning activities, responding to instructor prompts, and productive effort throughout
- Chatter that is directly related to the content
- Persistence in learning, even when it is hard
- Effort that is purposeful toward meeting learning goals
- Belief that the learning experiences and topic are important and relevant
- Genuine interest toward the topic and the learning experiences

Indications of students who are not engaged include the following:

- Passivity, distracting themselves and others, procrastination, avoidance of activities
- Depression or helplessness
- Active blocking of learning experiences for themselves and others
- Absenteeism or dropout

Engagement is achieved by (1) connecting learning experiences with student's goals and interests, and (2) by establishing sincere, caring relationships with students. Connecting learning experiences to student goals and interests is commonly achieved by increasing student agency—i.e., giving students increased control over learning. But choice is not enough. Student agency is only effective at increasing engagement when the available choices are of interest to students and appropriate to their ability. Relevance is the key. Establishing caring relationships with students is achieved by building trust, demonstrating concern for student success and well-being, expressing appropriate support and affirmation (and occasional tough love), and dialoguing with students on topics ranging from sensitive personal matters to subjects of humor and fun.

It takes effort, planning, and practice to engage students. Masters of engagement deliver with style, weave compelling narratives, and continuously look for and address indicators of disengagement. It is, in fact, meaningless to speak about the effectiveness of teachers, pedagogies, principles, technologies, or learning generally without also considering engagement: If students aren't engaged, nothing can be effective.

See also Parent Engagement; Social-Emotional Learning; Student-Teacher Relationship

Handbook of Research on Student Engagement by Sandra Christenson et al., (Eds.), 2012, Springer; "Analyzing Profiles, Predictors, and Consequences of Student Engagement Dispositions" by Michael Lawson and Katherine Masyn, *Journal of School Psychology*, 2015, 53, 63–86.

✓ DO

- Do link content and activities to student interests, backgrounds, and goals.
- Do take a personal interest in students, developing individual relationships when possible.
- Do provide students with a sense of ownership over their learning.
- Do test how different kinds of learning activities engage students and be flexible to change when needed.
- Do monitor and measure engagement over time—for example, by taking and reviewing videos of lessons for evidence of engagement or asking an experienced observer to monitor for signs of engagement.

✗ DON'T

- Don't allow students to give up.
- Don't mistake compliance for engagement.
- Don't punish students who show signs of disengagement, alienation, passivity, or helplessness—engage them.
- Don't provide only one progression through a course, or only one way for students to express their mastery of the content.
- Don't use extrinsic rewards such as grades or candy.
- Don't blame students for not being engaged.

❝ REFLECT

Contrary to what we usually believe, moments like these, the best moments in our lives, are not the passive, receptive, relaxing times—although such experiences can also be enjoyable, if we have worked hard to attain them. The best moments usually occur when a person's body or mind is stretched to its limits in a voluntary effort to accomplish something difficult and worthwhile. Optimal experience is thus something that we make happen.

—Mihaly Csikszentmihalyi

Flow: The Psychology of Optimal Experience by Mihaly Csikszentmihalyi, 2008, Harper Perennial Modern Classics.

19 Errors

An action, or omission of action, that yields an unintended result.

Identifying and remediating student errors is one of the core functions of teachers. But not all errors are equally serious, and not all strategies to correct them are equally effective. Additionally, the way a teacher treats student errors can determine whether students learn to embrace difficult challenges, or whether they become risk averse and avoid them. The first step toward addressing student errors is to understand the types and causes of errors, of which there are four types: slips, lapses, mistakes, and violations.

Slips, also referred to as errors of commission, occur when an action is not what was intended. With slips, students have the requisite knowledge or skill to perform a task, but accidentally commit an error while performing it. For example, a student knows the proper spelling of a word, but accidentally types it incorrectly. In this case of slips, self-correction is preferred. The student is presumed to know the correct response, and so teachers or peers should do no more than bring attention of the slip to the student.

Lapses, also referred to as errors of omission, occur when an action is missed due to a lapse of attention or memory. With lapses, students may have the requisite knowledge or skill to perform a task but have forgotten the answer or missed it due to distraction. For example, a student has difficulty recalling an answer to questions when placed in a stressful testing environment. In the case of lapses, the remedial strategy depends on the root cause. Lapses in memory suggest more practice is required, whereas lapses in attention suggest a change to the environment may be required (e.g., noise reduction).

Mistakes, also referred to as errors of intention, occur when an intention is incorrect. With mistakes, students are either guessing or believe they know the correct answer but are incorrect. For example, a student fails to find a common denominator before adding fractions with unlike denominators. In the case of mistakes, the student either has an incorrect understanding or lacks knowledge altogether. For minor misunderstandings, peer correction is an effective remedy. For major misunderstandings or gaps in knowledge, teacher correction is required. In both cases, mistakes tend to be symptomatic of wider-spread misunderstandings and are therefore ideal for sharing with the class.

Violations occur when an action deliberately breaks the rules or norms of conduct. Violations often appear to be errors but are distinct in that students knowingly and deliberately break the rules. For example, a student cheats on a homework assignment. Addressing violations should be handled with care. Rule violations with ill intent are cause for disciplinary action, but clever interpretations of rules and system hacks, assuming good intentions, are cause for sharing and celebration.

See also   Classroom Design; Creativity; Feedback; Peer Tutoring; Performance Load

---

Human Error by James Reason, 1990, Cambridge University Press; *A Life in Error* by James Reason, 2013, Routledge; *Teaching Language in Context: Proficiency-Oriented Instruction* by Alice Omaggio, 1986, Heinle.

DO ···

- ◆ Do create a culture that views errors as a natural part of the learning process.
- ◆ Do consider the types of errors students make and apply appropriate error correction strategies.
- ◆ Do have students self-correct slips.
- ◆ Do investigate the cause of lapses and consider the impact of environmental factors on attention and memory.
- ◆ Do encourage peer review and correction for minor mistakes.
- ◆ Do share and review major mistakes with the class, as they present teachable moments and typically indicate widespread misunderstanding.
- ◆ Do celebrate (however quietly) creative violations when made with good intent.

 DON'T ···

- ◆ Don't employ a monolithic error correction strategy.
- ◆ Don't embarrass or stigmatize those who make errors.
- ◆ Don't be too quick to punish violations made with good intent.

 REFLECT ···

Do we want to raise children to become adults who avoid challenging situations for fear of making mistakes? Did you give up on doing the laundry after you shrunk your favorite wool sweater? Did you stop offering ideas at the office when your last one didn't pan out? If learning from errors is not only possible but also a particularly effective learning tool, why not use this tool more often in schools? Many of our children could come to see the world through Edison's eyes, "Many of life's failures are people who did not realize how close they were to success when they gave up."

—Roberta Michnick Golinkoff and Kathy Hirsh-Pasek

"To Err Is Human, to Reflect (on the Error) Is Divine" by Roberta Michnick Golinkoff and Kathy Hirsh-Pasek, *Huffington Post*, April 24, 2017.

20 Executive Functions

A set of mental processes needed for purposeful, goal-oriented behavior.

Executive functions are a set of interrelated mental processes used to concentrate and pay attention. As a set, they account for more than twice the variation in final grades than IQ and can be developed throughout life, though longer-term benefits are most easily achieved in childhood. Executive functions are essential for developing mental and physical health, success in school and careers, and social and psychological well-being. Developing executive functions early is critical because the problems associated with deficits tend to amplify over time. There are three executive functions that form the foundation for all higher-order thinking processes such as reasoning, problem solving, and planning: working memory, cognitive flexibility, and inhibitory control.

Working memory is the mental whiteboard of the mind where new information is temporarily stored and manipulated. It is essential for recalling lists and sequences, mental problem solving, and relating new things to existing ideas. The general human limit of working memory is 4 ± 1 chunks—i.e., people can hold four to five new things in mind when first introduced to them. While working memory can be marginally improved through specific computer-based training programs (e.g., CogMed®) and curricula (e.g., PATHS™), these improvements do not appear to generalize or contribute to academic achievement. If there is a way to increase working memory generally, it likely requires a duration and intensity of practice that exceeds the scope of current research.

Cognitive flexibility is the ability to think creatively, change perspectives, and adapt to new rules and constraints. It is essential for empathizing with others, considering alternative approaches and ideas, changing one's mind and course when needed, multitasking, and supporting creative pursuits of all kinds. Cognitive flexibility can be developed through long-duration, high-intensity practice of activities requiring empathy, critical thinking, and creativity. For example, reading literary fiction and writing exercises that practice perspective taking of characters have been successful at significantly increasing both empathy and creativity.

Inhibitory control is the ability to control one's attention, behavior, thoughts, and emotions. It is essential for resisting temptation, delaying gratification, and overriding impulsive tendencies. Children with low inhibitory control grow up to have worse health, earn less money, be less happy, and commit more crimes than children with high inhibitory control. Even small improvements in inhibitory control in early childhood can yield large gains later in life. Inhibitory control can similarly be developed through long-duration, high-intensity practice of activities involving delayed response, if-then planning, self-discipline, stress reduction, and extended concentration.

See also Chunking; Creativity; Deliberate Practice; Intelligence; Metacognition

"Conclusions About Interventions, Programs, and Approaches for Improving Executive Functions that Appear Justified and Those That, Despite Much Hype, Do Not" by Adele Diamond, *Developmental Cognitive Neuroscience*, April 2016, 18, 34–48.

DO ···

- ◆ Do educate students about executive functions.
- ◆ Do frequently change learning activities, requiring students to continuously adapt and switch their approaches and mindsets.
- ◆ Do have students practice components of empathy (e.g., perspective taking), creativity (e.g., idea generation), and critical thinking (e.g., identifying biases) to develop cognitive flexibility.
- ◆ Do have students practice delayed response (e.g., wait three seconds before responding), if-then planning, self-discipline, and stress reduction to develop inhibitory control.
- ◆ Do engage students in activities that involve extended concentration, like chess and playing musical instruments.
- ◆ Do favor athletic activities that involve aerobic activity, concentration, and self-discipline, like martial arts, yoga, and social dance.
- ◆ Do incorporate executive function training into the curriculum.
- ◆ Do make executive function programs long term and high intensity—i.e., requiring conscious effort near the edge of student ability—beginning in early childhood and extending through adolescence.

DON'T ···

- ◆ Don't spend time developing working memory unless students have established working memory deficits (e.g., Attention-Deficit/Hyperactivity Disorder).
- ◆ Don't engage in "thoughtless" aerobic exercise (e.g., running on a treadmill) or general physical education to improve executive functions.
- ◆ Don't rely on brain-training games or software to increase executive functions—the gains do not generalize.

REFLECT ···

Whether EF gains are seen depends on the way in which an activity is done and the amount of time one spends doing it, pushing oneself to do better. It's the discipline, the practice, that produces the benefits. The most important element of a program might be that it involves an activity children love, so they will devote intensive time and effort to it. An enthusiastic, charismatic adult can often engender that passionate interest in children. Improving EFs and thus school and job success is serious business, yet there is no reason one needs to be grim though working hard on important matters; one can be joyful even while working hard.

—Adele Diamond

"Activities and Programs That Improve Children's Executive Functions" by Adele Diamond, *Current Directions in Psychological Science*, 2012, 21(5), 335–341.

21 Exercise Effects

Improved cognitive functioning that results from specific types of physical activity.

Exercise can be a significant contributor to learning, aiding cognitive function, mood regulation, and general mental health. But not all forms of exercise are equal. In terms of academic gains, aerobic activities (i.e., any activity that increases breathing and gets the heart beating fast for an extended period) are superior to activities focused on strength or flexibility. The same is true of sports—i.e., only those that involve aerobic activity are likely to produce learning benefits. Sports like golf, baseball, weightlifting, etc., offer many other kinds of benefits, but promoting cognitive function is not one of them. The key mechanism seems to regard the production of growth factors triggered by aerobic exercise, which in turn promotes the development of neural connections and blood vessels in the brain.

Consistency and duration both matter. Students who participate in an average of 15 minutes of moderate aerobic exercise a day improve their academic performance, with diminishing benefits after 60 minutes. However, consistency is more important than the total amount, so exercising 15 minutes daily is better than 75 minutes on Friday. And when this consistency is maintained over the long term, there is suggestive evidence that it can prevent or at least delay the onset of Alzheimer's and dementia.

Exercising before versus after learning is preferable, so it is better for students to exercise in the morning or mid-day. Some schools have even found the introduction of small exercise breaks and increasing recess time to be effective in addressing behavioral and attention-related problems such as Attention-Deficit/Hyperactivity-Disorder. Exercise at the end of a school day does not appear to benefit learning.

New research suggests benefits similar to aerobic exercise might be achieved through High-Intensity Training (i.e., brief bursts of maximal-effort workout followed by short periods of rest, repeated for a minimum of seven minutes). Doing High-Intensity Training three times a week may be an even more efficient way to gain cognitive benefits, but this research is still in the early stages.

Exercise effects should be considered in the design of all school schedules. The hours in a school day are limited, which means that time spent exercising necessarily results in less instructional time. However, a 15-minute reduction in instructional time has a nominal negative impact on academic achievement, whereas a 15-minute addition of aerobic activity has a significant positive impact across all classes. In this quality versus quantity tradeoff, improved quality of learning trumps reduced quantity of instruction.

See also Classroom Management; Executive Functions; Play; Sleep Strategies

"Exercise and Children's Intelligence, Cognition, and Academic Achievement" by Phillip Tomporowski et al., *Educational Psychology Review*, 2008, 20(2), 111–131; "Effects of Physical Exercise on Cognitive Functioning and Wellbeing: Biological and Psychological Benefits" by Laura Mandolesi et al., *Frontiers in Psychology*, 2018, 9, article 509.

DO ···

- ◆ Do have students exercise a minimum of 15 minutes a day multiple times a week.
- ◆ Do encourage students to exercise during breaks.
- ◆ Do include moderate aerobic exercise before classes when possible.
- ◆ Do prioritize aerobic exercise during physical education classes, considering also High-Intensity Interval Training and High-Intensity Training.
- ◆ Do favor extracurricular sports options that emphasize aerobic activities.
- ◆ Do provide exercise opportunities throughout the day in the form of breaks and recess.
- ◆ Do teach students about the cognitive benefits of exercise.

 DON'T ···

- ◆ Don't focus on strength-building or flexibility activities when learning is the goal.
- ◆ Don't make exercise so intense that it distracts students from learning.
- ◆ Don't punish students by limiting exercise opportunities, such as taking away recess.
- ◆ Don't do extended exercise sessions infrequently (e.g., once per week).
- ◆ Don't promote or invest significant resources in sports that lack an aerobic component.

❝ REFLECT ···

We need to have kids moving every day, not just because it makes sense health-wise, but because it raises test scores.

—John Ratey

"Studies Show the Long-Term, Positive Effects of Fitness on Cognitive Abilities" by Christie Aschwanden and New Scientist, *The Washington Post*, December 9, 2013.

22 Expectation Effects

A change in behavior or performance that results from a change in beliefs.

Expectations can shape outcomes. They often lead to behaviors that cause expectations to be realized, resulting in a self-fulfilling prophecy. Expectations held by students, teachers, and parents can all impact achievement and socioemotional health, making this phenomenon important to recognize. Expectation effects that impact education take a variety of forms, including the following:

- Growth mindset: When students believe that intelligence is not fixed, they work harder to achieve academically.
- Pygmalion effect: When teachers believe that a student or group of students is more intelligent than another, they unconsciously favor them.
- Golem effect: When students internalize systematically lowered expectations, their performance declines.
- Halo effect: When teachers have positive impressions of a student, they evaluate that student more positively.
- Labeling effect: When students are labeled, their achievement may be elevated or reduced due to associations with the label.
- Attribution error: When performance is attributed to internal factors like genetics or personality, external factors like teacher or school quality are underestimated.

When expectations are easily falsifiable (e.g., sugar pills cure cancer), expectation effects tend to be small and dissipate over time. But when expectations are not easily falsifiable and reinforced by authority figures, social norms, and institutional practices, expectation effects can be large with lasting consequences. For example, in Jane Elliott's classic blue-eyed/brown-eyed experiment, third-grade children were told that eye color determined their behavior and intelligence. She told the class that blue-eyed children were smart and good and brown-eyed children were bad and dumb, and both groups began to behave accordingly: Blue-eyed children were better behaved and performed better academically than their brown-eyed classmates. When Elliot informed the class that she had made a mistake and that it was actually the brown-eyed children who were smart and good, the behaviors and performance of both groups reversed in short order. When people sincerely believe in something that is reinforced by authority and not easily falsifiable, this alone can make it so. Such effects are larger among students who are young or from marginalized groups, which underscores the perils of common practices like ability grouping and labeling.

See also   Ability Grouping; Engagement, Student; Metacognition; Motivation

"Teacher Expectations and Self-fulfilling Prophecies: Knowns and Unknowns, Resolved and Unresolved Controversies" by Lee Jussim and Kent Harber, *Personality and Social Psychology Review*, 2005, 9(2), 131–155; "Are Teachers' Expectations Different for Racial Minority than for European American Students? A Meta-Analysis" by Harriet Tenenbaum and Martin Ruck, *Journal of Educational Psychology*, 2007, 99(2), 253–273.

DO ···

- ◆ Do set high expectations for students.
- ◆ Do leverage expectation effects that push students to achieve their maximum potential.
- ◆ Do educate students, parents, and colleagues about the risks, benefits, and limits of expectation effects.
- ◆ Do take measures to mitigate potential biases when interacting, evaluating, and rewarding/punishing students.
- ◆ Do focus feedback on individual effort and positive behaviors, and away from abilities and performance relative to others.
- ◆ Do emphasize expectations of progress over perfection—i.e., getting better over becoming best.

 DON'T ··

- ◆ Don't label students or groups based on ability or achievement.
- ◆ Don't create schedules, classes, or school policies that systematize lowered expectations for students.
- ◆ Don't rely only on high expectations to close achievement gaps and fail to address structural or systemic problems.

 REFLECT ··

I use phonics. We use the card pack, and the children, the brown-eyed children were in the low class the first day and it took them five and a half minutes to get through the card pack. The second day it took them two and a half minutes. The only thing that had changed was the fact that now they were superior people.

—Jane Elliott

"A Class Divided" by William Peters, *PBS Frontline*, March 26, 1985.

23 Feedback

Information provided to students about their performance relative to their goals.

Feedback is an essential element of learning—without feedback of some kind, learning cannot occur. Therefore, it should come as no surprise that the efficiency of learning is inextricably linked to the effectiveness of the feedback provided during a learning experience. The question is what constitutes effective feedback?

There are many taxonomies and models of feedback, but effective feedback can be reduced to two basic types, directive and facilitative, each with their own benefits, caveats, and guidelines. Directive feedback provides clear, actionable information that identifies correct responses, errors, and misconceptions. By contrast, facilitative feedback provides clues, suggestions, and hints so the student can identify their own progress and gaps. It also prevents the student from becoming reliant on directive feedback.

Directive feedback is best suited for novice students, students with low motivation, or difficult tasks. It works best for factual, procedural, and conceptual goals, and should be delivered to students as quickly as possible. Facilitative feedback is best suited for self-regulated, advanced students, and students with high motivation. It works best for transfer of learning to new contexts, abstract concepts, and metacognitive goals, and should be delivered after a delay to allow students to reflect on their work and growth before receiving feedback.

Feedback that causes students to focus on themselves, or compare themselves to other students, should be avoided. Feedback that can be perceived as threatening to students' conceptions of themselves decreases motivation. And feedback that doesn't help students understand what they don't know, such as general praise or punishment, is unproductive and can actually have a negative impact on learning. The key question is what will help students do things that they couldn't do before receiving the feedback? Answering this question requires a lot of listening. Studies of classrooms worldwide indicate that teachers talk between 80–95 percent of the time, leaving little time to listen, assess student knowledge, and provide appropriate feedback.

For all of the teachers who have dutifully stayed up all night writing extensive feedback for their students, there is good news: less is more. Feedback that is extensive or tangential has little corrective benefit and reduces motivation. The best feedback dosage provides just enough information to guide the student toward the goal. Limiting feedback to one or two points that enable students to take the next steps is best.

See also Assessment, Formative; Assessment, Summative; Direct Instruction; Errors

"Focus on Formative Feedback" by Valerie Schute, *Review of Educational Research*, 2008, 78(1), 153–189. For a popular treatment, see *How to Give Effective Feedback to Your Students* (2nd ed.) by Susan Brookhart, 2017, Association for Supervision & Curriculum Development.

DO ···

- ◆ Do compare student work to learning targets to provide the most effective feedback.
- ◆ Do provide immediate directive feedback to beginner students.
- ◆ Do provide delayed feedback to advanced students and when transfer of learning is the goal.
- ◆ Do favor clues and suggestions to advanced students so that they can evaluate themselves and determine next steps.
- ◆ Do provide students the opportunity to implement feedback.
- ◆ Do limit feedback to one or two points to enable students to take the next steps in their learning.

 DON'T ···

- ◆ Don't overwhelm students with too much feedback.
- ◆ Don't provide feedback that is about students themselves as opposed to their work or approach.
- ◆ Don't provide feedback that compares students to other students.
- ◆ Don't rely on feedback that generalizes performance in a comparative way (e.g., letter grades or percentages).
- ◆ Don't use non-specific praise or criticism in feedback.
- ◆ Don't stay up all night writing extensive feedback for students.

❝ REFLECT ···

When teachers spend hours and hours writing comments, if there's no feedback providing concrete steps for the students to improve, students will argue themselves blue in the face that they never received anything. The key question is, does feedback help someone understand what they don't know, what they do know, and where they go? That's when and why feedback is so powerful, but a lot of feedback doesn't—and doesn't have any effect.

—John Hattie

"Getting Feedback Right: A Q&A With John Hattie" by Sarah Sparks, *Education Week*, June 19, 2018.

24 Flexibility Tradeoffs

As the flexibility of a design increases, performance of the design decreases.

There is an inherent tradeoff in the design of all systems between flexibility and performance: Accommodating flexibility entails satisfying a larger set of design requirements, which invariably means compromises in the design. For example, take the Swiss Army knife. It has more tools and hence greater flexibility than an individual knife, corkscrew, screwdriver, or saw, but combining these tools into one requires compromises in their design that reduce their performance. If one needs a high performing screwdriver, a standalone screwdriver would be preferred. However, if one needs to be prepared for a range of possibilities, the flexibility of a Swiss Army knife is preferred. The goal determines whether specialization or flexibility is the best choice. A design can be optimized for flexibility or performance, but not both.

Flexibility tradeoffs apply to the design of all systems, including those in education. Students graduating from a very specialized curriculum (e.g., vocational school) will perform better in the area of specialization than students graduating from a very broad curriculum (e.g., liberal arts school), but the liberal arts students will outperform the vocational students in a wider range of environments. Similarly, all things being equal, a school that exclusively teaches to a standardized test will produce students that score higher on that test than other schools, but the tradeoff is that their students will perform less well in all other areas.

So how to choose between performance and flexibility? Specialized designs outperform flexible designs when their requirements are stable. Flexible designs outperform specialized designs when their requirements are volatile. In other words, if a school is graduating students into environments that are well defined and stable, specialized educational designs should be favored. The curricular focus would be on mastering the content and skills specific to success in the defined target environment. However, if a school is graduating students into environments that are ill-defined and volatile, broad educational designs should be favored. The curricular focus in these cases would be on more generalized thinking and problem-solving skills and less on content-specific skills.

In most learning contexts, the choice is not either-or, but a decision about where on the performance-flexibility continuum students should be. For example, schools that commit to intensive college prep do so to improve their student's prospects at college admissions, but their increased performance in college admissions comes at a cost to their practical and general education. Conversely, schools that commit to a pure educational philosophy and resist college prep improve their students' general knowledge and adaptivity, but their increased flexibility comes at a cost of being less competitive in college admissions. There are those that claim you can have both—give them a Swiss Army knife.

See also   80/20 Rule; Decision Making; Study Tactics; Transfer

Universal Principles of Design by William Lidwell et al., 2010, Rockport Publishers; *The Pocket Universal Principles of Design* by William Lidwell et al., 2015, Rockport Publishers.

✅ DO

- Do reflect on the goal of the educational program and be intentional about flexibility-performance tradeoffs in its design.
- Do narrow the scope of curricula and educational designs when the target environment is well defined and stable (e.g., vocational school training students to become diesel mechanics).
- Do broaden the scope of curricula and educational designs when the target environment is ill defined and volatile (e.g., liberal arts school preparing students for an uncertain future).
- Do consider that increasing flexibility increases complexity, which typically increases cost.
- Do believe the old aphorism, "Jack of all trades, master of none, but oftentimes better than master of one."

❌ DON'T

- Don't be deceived into believing that flexibility can be increased without trading off performance.
- Don't expect broad educational programs to perform well on specialized measures, nor expect specialized educational programs to perform well on broad measures.

💬 REFLECT

There is great appeal to the idea that you can design something flexibly to perform many different functions, at less cost, and at a greater level of performance than more specialized designs. It is the siren song of design. But unless existing specialized designs are just terribly inefficient, this idea is always wrong. And flexibility tradeoffs are the reason why.

—William Lidwell

"Universal Principles of Design: Flexibility Tradeoffs" by William Lidwell and Jill Butler, *LinkedIn Learning*, July 19, 2017, www.linkedin.com/learning/universal-principles-of-design/flexibility-trade-offs.

25 Homework

Activities assigned to support in-class instruction that takes place outside of the classroom.

The debate around homework burns hot. Advocates argue that homework provides essential opportunities to practice skills, prepare for upcoming lessons, and extend learning to new contexts. Critics argue that the benefits of homework in practice are outweighed by their costs: increased stress, reduced playtime, disrupted sleep, and strains on the parent-child relationship. What is the evidence?

In general, the upper limit of homework assigned should not exceed 10 minutes multiplied by the grade level per night—for example, 60 minutes per night for sixth grade, 90 minutes per night for ninth grade, and so on. This is referred to as the "ten-minute" rule. Beyond this limit, student achievement declines. For elementary grades, however, the achievement gains of homework are small, and the socioemotional costs are high. Therefore, homework in these early grades is counterproductive and should be avoided. Non-traditional forms of homework—e.g., student-directed projects—may fare better, but the research is still inconclusive. For middle and upper grades, homework is positively linked to student achievement and performance on standardized tests. The gains appear strongest when homework is evenly distributed throughout the week and followed by teacher feedback. When homework is assigned irregularly or en masse, achievement is negatively impacted.

In terms of type, homework assignments that emphasize practice, preparation, and extension can all be effective, though activities that engage students to extend what they have learned to new contexts and situations produce the greatest gains. It should be noted, however, that homework of any type, assuming moderate-to-good quality, appears better than no homework at all. Stated simply: Good but imperfect homework is better than no homework, but no homework is better than busywork.

School surveys on homework frequency and duration indicate that schools assign too much homework (of both good and bad quality). The costs of this excess are amplified when teachers fail to coordinate their homework assignments, and when students are engaged in extracurricular activities, such as sports and clubs. Accordingly, developing and enforcing a comprehensive school policy to align homework practice with the research evidence is a low-cost, high-benefit means of improving student academic achievement and socioemotional well-being.

See also Interleaving; Parent Engagement; Social-Emotional Learning; Spacing

---

"Does Homework Improve Academic Achievement? A Synthesis of Research, 1987–2003" by Harris Cooper et al., *Review of Educational Research*, 2006, 76(1), 1–62; "The Homework-Achievement Relation Reconsidered: Differentiating Homework Time, Homework Frequency, and Homework Effort" by Ulrich Trautwein, *Learning and Instruction*, 2007, 17(3), 372–388. For a critical perspective of the homework research, see *The Homework Myth: Why Our Kids Get Too Much of a Bad Thing* by Alfie Kohn, 2006, Cambridge, MA: Da Capo Press.

DO ···

- ◆ Do follow the ten-minute rule (except in elementary school).
- ◆ Do assign homework in regular and consistent amounts (e.g., daily, ten problems) throughout the week.
- ◆ Do provide feedback on homework in class.
- ◆ Do encourage students to complete homework independently, seeking help only when needed.
- ◆ Do favor homework that extends learning to new contexts and situations over practice and preparation.
- ◆ Do coordinate with other teachers to ensure the total amount of homework assigned is within recommended limits.

 DON'T ··

- ◆ Don't assign traditional homework to students in elementary school.
- ◆ Don't assign busywork or use homework to punish students.
- ◆ Don't assign homework in massed amounts—e.g., one five-hour homework assignment one day a week versus a one-hour assignment each day.
- ◆ Don't assign homework just to assign homework. Homework needs to be meaningful and engaging to be effective.
- ◆ Don't compromise opportunities for students to participate in extracurricular activities in order to assign more homework.

REFLECT ···

Too much homework not only crowds out time for other activities and increases stress on kids but there is no evidence that those last three hours of a five hour homework binge accomplishes what it set out to do, improve learning.

—Harris Cooper

"Homework's Diminishing Returns" by Harris Cooper in "The Opinion Pages: Room for Debate," *The New York Times*, December 12, 2010.

26 Intelligence

The general capability to comprehend, problem solve, reason, and learn.

Despite the controversy that surrounds intelligence, it is the most researched, validated, and reliably measured construct in the psychological sciences. It is strongly associated with a variety of positive lifetime outcomes, including career success, health, longevity, beneficial relationships, and more. So why isn't everyone in education working around the clock to understand and seek ways to improve intelligence? Perhaps because many educators believe that intelligence is genetically determined and therefore immutable. Let's consider the evidence.

Twin and family studies coupled with genomic studies indicate that genetics explains about half of general intelligence; the remaining half is explained by the environment, which includes education. And it turns out that the most effective method known to raise general intelligence is increasing the number of years of schooling, which results in IQ gains of roughly one to five points per year. This is big news for educators, and may explain why general intelligence has been increasing by about 3 IQ points per decade for the last 100 years, a phenomenon known as the Flynn effect.

Detailed research into the educational approaches that are most effective at increasing intelligence is ongoing, but education likely raises intelligence in two ways: (1) expanding skills, knowledge, and experience, resulting in gains in crystallized intelligence and (2) practicing reasoning and problem-solving skills in a variety of novel contexts over long periods of time, resulting in gains in fluid intelligence.

The bottom line is that intelligence is not fixed, and the best way to increase it is through education. As researchers uncover approaches and opportunities that are more effective at increasing intelligence, savvy teachers will take note and avoid falling through the trapdoors of misunderstanding and controversy, and their students will benefit.

Let's conclude by debunking a few prevalent intelligence myths:

- IQ tests just measure how good people are at taking IQ tests. FALSE
- Playing Mozart for babies makes them smarter. FALSE
- Brain-training games increase intelligence. FALSE
- Humans use only 10 percent of their brains. FALSE
- There are seven (or more) specialized types of intelligence. FALSE
- There is an emotional intelligence (EQ). FALSE

See also Deliberate Practice; Executive Functions; Expectation Effects; Transfer

Intelligence: All That Matters by Stuart Ritchie, 2015, John Murray Learning; "Multiple Intelligences, the Mozart Effect, and Emotional Intelligence: A Critical Review" by Lynn Waterhouse, *Educational Psychologist*, 2006, 41(4), 207–225; "Intelligence: New Findings and Theoretical Developments" by Richard Nisbett et al., *The American Psychologist*, 2012, 67(2), 130–159.

DO ∙∙∙

- ◆ Do encourage students to stay in school and pursue post-secondary education.
- ◆ Do provide opportunities for students to enhance their executive functions, especially during early childhood.
- ◆ Do provide opportunities for students to practice reasoning and problem-solving abilities in different ways.
- ◆ Do integrate modeling abstract systems into classes such as math, science, and logic.
- ◆ Do encourage students to continuously challenge themselves to learn new things in novel contexts.
- ◆ Do encourage participation in summer learning programs.
- ◆ Do try to mitigate risk factors that students face, such as chronic stress, drug use, obesity, and lack of family support.

 DON'T ∙∙

- ◆ Don't promote common intelligence myths.
- ◆ Don't support student experimentation with "smart drugs" or transcranial direct current stimulation (tDCS).
- ◆ Don't use IQ test practice or prep to raise intelligence.
- ◆ Don't categorize or treat students differently based on intelligence test results.
- ◆ Don't disregard the study of intelligence and its development because it is controversial.

REFLECT ∙∙∙

Certainly, the next time you see a technique, game, supplement or pill that claims to boost your brainpower, regard it with extreme skepticism. Nevertheless, we're lucky that the tools for raising intelligence—which might partly have caused the Flynn effect—seem to be staring us in the face, in the form of education. Now, intelligence researchers have to find out exactly how education has these effects, and how we can make the most of them.

—Stuart Ritchie

Intelligence: All that Matters by Stuart Ritchie, 2015, John Murray Learning.

27 Interleaving
Mixing different types of learning activities to promote skill proficiency, memory retention, and transfer.

Given the option of practicing one type of activity over and over (known as blocking or massing) or practicing a random mix of related activities (known as interleaving), the latter results in superior learning in most contexts. For example, students learn more effectively when solving a mix of related problems (e.g., volumetric problems mixing cones, spheres, pyramids, and cubes) versus solving blocks of just one kind of problem (e.g., volumetric problems of cubes). The performance gains of this type of practice are significant: up to two to three times when measured after a few days, and the gains increase over time.

Why does interleaving work? What is the operating mechanism? Blocked practice allows students to get into a mode of thoughtless repetition, applying the same problem-solving strategy over and over. Interleaving avoids this, requiring students to continuously discriminate problem types and then consciously select the appropriate problem-solving strategy. This specific type of extra mental effort—problem discrimination and strategy selection—seems to be the key to interleaving. Therefore, three conditions must be satisfied for students to benefit from interleaving:

1. The problems or tasks practiced must be similar to one another. For example, mixing related types of math problems would benefit students, whereas mixing math problems and writing exercises would not.
2. Discriminating between the types of problems or tasks must require effortful problem discrimination and strategy selection. For example, when it is easy to distinguish between categories (e.g., mammals vs. plants vs. bugs), interleaving and blocking are equally effective; when it is difficult to distinguish (e.g., types of birds), interleaving is more effective.
3. Students must have sufficient prior knowledge and skills to be able to practice before interleaving can be used. For novices and young children, blocking is more effective.

It is worth noting that even when the aforementioned conditions are satisfied, students overwhelmingly perceive that they learn more effectively with blocked versus interleaved practice. Despite these perceptions, the evidence is clear: Interleaved practice is far superior to blocked practice in most contexts. And new research suggests that it not only increases long-term skill proficiency and memory retention, it also facilitates transfer to new contexts. But these gains come at a cost: Interleaved practice is harder and perceived progress is slower. So remind your students: no pain, no gain.

See also   Depth of Processing; Retrieval Practice; Scaffolding; Spacing; Transfer

"Learning Concepts and Categories: Is Spacing the 'Enemy of Induction?'" by Nate Kornell and Robert Bjork, *Psychological Science*, 2008, 19(6), 585–592; "The Benefits of Interleaved Practice for Learning" by Sean HK Kang *From the Laboratory to the Classroom: Translating Science of Learning for Teachers* by Jared Cooney et al. (Ed.), 2016, Routledge, 91–105.

DO ···

- Do intersperse practice with different but related skills.
- Do make problem and task types similar enough to require conscious discrimination and strategy selection.
- Do ensure that each problem and task type gets sufficient practice, at least ten activities per skill.
- Do use both new and previously learned activities when interleaving exercises.
- Do use blocked practice to develop foundational skills and knowledge, and then transition to interleaved practice.
- Do remind and encourage students: no pain, no gain.

 **DON'T** ···

- Don't interleave problems or tasks that are highly dissimilar.
- Don't interleave practice when students have minimal skill or knowledge relevant to the topic.
- Don't use interleaving with young children.
- Don't accept anecdotes or self-reports that blocked practice is more effective.

REFLECT ···

It's widely believed by teachers, trainers, and coaches that the most effective way to master a new skill is to give it dogged, single-minded focus, practicing over and over until you've got it down. Our faith in this runs deep, because most of us see fast gains during the learning phase of massed practice. What's apparent from the research is that gains achieved during massed practice are transitory and melt away quickly.

—Peter Brown

Make It Stick: The Science of Successful Learning by Peter Brown, Henry Roediger III, and Mark McDaniel, 2014, The Belknap Press.

28 Metacognition

Knowledge of one's own thinking that leads to increased academic success.

While intelligence enables students to think and learn well, their metacognitive ability enables them to think and learn better. Metacognition has three main components: knowledge, monitoring, and control. Metacognitive knowledge refers to a person's knowledge about thinking, about how the brain works, and about which study tactics work and which don't. This book, for example, is chock-full of metacognitive knowledge. Metacognitive monitoring refers to a person's ability to evaluate their own thinking, to know when they know and when they don't know something, and to detect bugs and biases in their thinking. Metacognitive control refers to a student's ability to consciously change their thinking, to alter their study tactics or their approach to problem solving, and to correct bugs and biases in their thinking. In general, students who develop their metacognitive ability perform about twice as well as students who don't.

Metacognitive monitoring is particularly challenging to develop, but as they say, recognition is the necessary first step to recovery. There can be no correction until there is recognition of a problem, and novices are poor at self-assessing their level of understanding. For example, it is well documented that novice learners—which includes most students—consistently overestimate their level of mastery. The path to correction is quality feedback on their self-assessments, which enables students to tune their monitoring and assess with increasing accuracy. But in the absence of such feedback, novices are "doubly cursed": They perform poorly while actually perceiving that they perform well, a phenomenon known as the Dunning-Kruger effect. And it turns out that knowledge about phenomena like the Dunning-Kruger helps to improve monitoring.

Metacognitive control requires both metacognitive knowledge and accurate monitoring; the former provides the toolbox of solutions and the latter provides the troubleshooting. When students have both metacognitive knowledge and monitoring, they are able to adapt their learning and achieve greater success. For example, teach one group of students problem-solving strategies and another group the same strategies with techniques to evaluate and adjust their thinking (e.g., self-quizzing and self-explanation), and research suggests that the latter group will solve problems twice as well and twice as fast.

It should be noted that metacognitive abilities change with age. For example, children below fourth grade tend to be overconfident in their ability to learn new things but are as accurate—sometimes even more accurate—than older children in judging the correctness of their learning. Teaching metacognitive monitoring is useful for students of all ages, but teaching strategies for metacognitive control should be delayed until primary school.

See also   Assessment, Self; Expectation Effects; Intelligence; Teach-to-Learn; Transfer

---

"Metacognition and Cognitive Monitoring: A New Area of Cognitive—Developmental Inquiry" by John Flavell, *American Psychologist*, 1979, 34(10), 906; *Metacognition* by John Dunlosky and Janet Metcalfe, 2008, Sage Publications, 200–232.

DO ··

- ◆ Do create time for students to reflect on their performance and to get feedback on the quality of that reflection.
- ◆ Do give students clear goals against which to monitor their learning and adjust their approach.
- ◆ Do offer students instruction about how people think, learn, and remember.
- ◆ Do equip students with subject-specific strategies that enable them to plan, monitor, evaluate, and adjust their learning.
- ◆ Do instruct knowledge and skills as an effective way to improve metacognition in subject domains.

DON'T ··

- ◆ Don't have students reflect without evaluating and providing feedback on the accuracy of their reflections.
- ◆ Don't assume that metacognition in one subject transfers automatically to another.
- ◆ Don't teach metacognitive control techniques such as study skills to students before primary school.
- ◆ Don't have students reflect on their learning without knowing the learning goal.

REFLECT ··

There is a need to teach for metacognitive knowledge explicitly . . . we are continually surprised at the number of students who come to college having very little metacognitive knowledge; knowledge about different strategies, different cognitive tasks, and particularly, accurate knowledge about themselves.

—Paul Pintrich

"The Role of Metacognitive Knowledge in Learning, Teaching, and Assessing" by Paul Pintrich, *Theory Into Practice*, Autumn 2002, 41(4), 219–225.

29 Mnemonic Devices

Techniques of organizing information to make that information easier to remember.

Mnemonic devices are memory-enhancing techniques that involve the use of imagery or words in specific ways to link familiar information to unfamiliar information. For example, acronym mnemonics use letters as cues to remember lists of words in a particular sequence, such as ROYGBIV for the colors of the rainbow. Mnemonics work for students of all ages and are especially beneficial for students with learning difficulties.

Mnemonic devices are useful for recalling large amounts of rote information, but there is suggestive evidence that they can support higher-order learning as well. For example, research on hierarchical reasoning and transfer tasks finds that students using mnemonics consistently outperform groups that do not. Note that specialized mnemonic devices used to recall one thing (e.g., "Red touch yellow, kills a fellow. Red touch black, friend of Jack" to distinguish coral snakes from non-venomous snakes) only aid the recall of a specific item. In contrast, general-purpose mnemonic devices can be used to recall anything. Three of the general-purpose variety stand out for their effectiveness: (1) chain method, (2) peg system, and (3) method of loci.

The chain method works by associating items in a list with one another in sequence, creating a kind of story chain. For example, to remember the items dog, bird, and house, visualize a dog catching a bird in its mouth and then running into the house. The peg system is a bit more involved. It links a list of concrete things to items in a known series, usually with rhyme, and then each concrete thing to a thing to be remembered. For example, begin with the number sequence 1, 2, 3. Add concrete items to each of these numbers through rhyme, such as 1-sun, 2-shoe, 3-bee. Then, for any three new items to be remembered, visualize them interacting with the concrete items. To remember the first three planets in the solar system, imagine Mercury hugging the sun, and Venus being stepped on by a giant shoe, and Earth being stung by a bee. The method of loci mnemonic works similarly, but instead of a known series, it uses familiar space (e.g., a student's house). People visualize placing objects at different locations in the space, and then the items are recalled by visualizing walking around the space.

Students trained in mnemonic techniques like these perform about twice as well on recall tests as students trained in traditional study methods. Additionally, research suggests that mnemonics incorporated into review sheets and study materials can make learning more effective and more enjoyable for students, while also reducing their test anxiety. Having students generate their own mnemonics adds to their recall strength and enjoyability, and so should be favored when possible.

See also Chunking; Depth of Processing; Dual Coding; Study Tactics

---

"The Effectiveness of Four Mnemonics in Ordering Recall" by Henry Roediger, *Journal of Experimental Psychology: Human Learning and Memory*, 1980, 6(5), 558–567; "Mnemonics in Education: Current Research and Applications" by Adam Putnam, *Translational Issues in Psychological Science*, 2015, 1(2), 130–139.

DO ···

- ◆ Do encourage students to develop their own specialized mnemonic devices for key material.
- ◆ Do consider training students in chain, peg, and loci mnemonics to aid general recall.
- ◆ Do favor mnemonic devices for students with special needs and memory challenges.
- ◆ Do have fun with mnemonics, exploring rhymes, music, caricatures, humor, etc.
- ◆ Do combine mnemonic devices with retrieval practice and other learning strategies to enhance long-term retention.

 DON'T ···

- ◆ Don't use mnemonics for everything. Reserve their use for foundational items intended for long-term recall.
- ◆ Don't use mnemonics when the speed of recall is important.
- ◆ Don't use mnemonic devices to teach nonsequential information or skills.
- ◆ Don't incorporate unfamiliar cues into mnemonic devices.

 REFLECT ··

The principles that the oral bards discovered, as they sharpened their stories through telling and retelling, were the same basic mnemonic principles that psychologists rediscovered when they began conducting their first scientific experiments on memory around the turn of the twentieth century: Words that rhyme are much more memorable than words that don't; concrete nouns are easier to remember than abstract nouns; dynamic images are more memorable than static images; alliteration aids memory. A striped skunk making a slam dunk is a stickier thought than a patterned mustelid engaging in athletic activity.

—Joshua Foer

Moonwalking With Einstein: The Art and Science of Remembering Everything by Joshua Foer, 2011, Penguin Press.

30 Motivation

The drive to engage in activities.

There are two types of motivation: intrinsic and extrinsic. Intrinsic motivation is the drive to engage in activities because a person finds them enjoyable. Extrinsic motivation is the drive to engage in activities because a person seeks to obtain a reward. A student reading a novel because they love reading is intrinsically motivated, whereas a student reading a novel for money is extrinsically motivated.

Learning is most effective when students are intrinsically motivated, especially when learning involves creativity and problem solving. Teachers can foster intrinsic motivation by ensuring that learning experiences include three qualities: autonomy, mastery, and purpose. Autonomy refers to giving students opportunities to make choices in the learning process. Mastery refers to giving students opportunities to get better at something that matters. Purpose refers to giving students opportunities to make a meaningful difference.

When intrinsic motivation is present, extrinsic rewards should be avoided. Extrinsic rewards undermine intrinsic motivation. However, intrinsic motivation often is not present, and the practical challenge is motivating students to do necessary but unexciting work. In such cases, extrinsic rewards can be used as a means of engagement and bridge to ultimately achieving intrinsic motivation. In such cases, it is critical to structure the incentives properly: Rewards should be used to engage students in behaviors related to learning versus rewarding them for achieving specific outcomes. For example, extrinsically rewarding behaviors like attendance, good conduct, wearing school uniforms, doing homework, and reading books can be very effective at improving learning, whereas extrinsically rewarding outcomes like grades and test results are ineffective. Applying rewards that are progressively small, intangible, and based on mastery can help students gain confidence and transition to becoming more intrinsically motivated. Keeping external rewards unexpected can also help prevent students from acting only because they expect the reward. This practice should be phased out quickly once intrinsic motivation becomes evident.

Relationships with teachers and peers powerfully impact motivation. It is therefore important that teachers and students value and acknowledge the role of autonomy, mastery, and purpose in the learning experience. This is true in all contexts, but particularly true in contexts where students have been demotivated by learning environments that prioritized control and compliance.

See also   Creativity; Engagement, Student; Feedback; Play; Student-Teacher Relationship

---

"Intrinsic and Extrinsic Motivations: Classic Definitions and New Directions" by Richard Ryan and Edward Deci, *Contemporary Educational Psychology*, 2000, 25, 54–67; For a popular treatment, see *Drive: The Surprising Truth About What Motivates Us* by Daniel Pink, 2011, Riverhead Books.

DO ··

- ◆ Do motivate students by engaging them to feel ownership in the learning process, creating time to pursue mastery, and designing activities where they serve purposes greater than themselves.
- ◆ Do use students' sense of accomplishment to motivate them.
- ◆ Do consider rewards to promote key learning-related behaviors, but phase them out so that students do not become dependent.
- ◆ Do emphasize student autonomy when extrinsic rewards are required.
- ◆ Do favor intangible rewards (such as positive verbal feedback) over tangible rewards (such as parties).
- ◆ Do recognize and leverage the role of positive relationships in intrinsic motivation.
- ◆ Do deemphasize rewards. The more prominent an extrinsic reward, the more likely intrinsic motivation will be undermined.

DON'T ···

- ◆ Don't use rewards when students are intrinsically motivated.
- ◆ Don't use rewards when tasks are complex, open-ended, or have unclear next steps.
- ◆ Don't use rewards to achieve complex outcomes.
- ◆ Don't use rewards (or punishments) for activities requiring intense concentration, creativity, or problem solving.
- ◆ Don't resort to control or coercion when students are not intrinsically motivated.

REFLECT ···

The whole field of motivation has changed over the last 40 years, from thinking about how you can control people from the outside to thinking how you can really facilitate and support people's commitment and engagement in activities.

—Richard Ryan

"The Right Kind of Motivation Comes From You" by Sandra Knispel, *Futurity*, June 23, 2017.

31 Peer Tutoring

Students helping other students to learn.

Peer tutoring, when done right, has large and widespread benefits on student learning. Student tutors learn more deeply by teaching the material, and student tutees learn by receiving feedback and social support in areas where they struggle. Both the student tutor and tutee gain in academic achievement relative to their non-tutored peers. For example, take a middle-ranked student from a class of 100 students. Have this student participate in a peer-tutoring program for 10 weeks as either a tutor or tutee, and research suggests their class ranking would improve by about 19 students.

Peer tutoring program generally pair students in one of three ways: same-age reciprocal (when similarly aged students act both as tutor and tutee), same-age nonreciprocal (when one student is the tutor to a similarly aged tutee), and cross-grade (when an older student is the tutor and a younger the tutee). Peer tutoring works best when students of different ability levels in a content area work together. For example, one student may be advanced in math and another in history, and they can tutor each other to mutual benefit. It is worth noting that these benefits not only extend to general student populations, but to students with learning challenges as well. As long as a gap in ability exists, all three forms of peer tutoring can be effective and enjoyable for students. For those considering peer tutoring, the following guidelines should be used:

1. Peer tutoring should not be used to teach new material, but only to help students develop proficiency with material they've been learning. Teachers should teach and tutors tutor.
2. In comparison to assigning pairs to work on a specific assignment, allowing the pairs to choose what they work on enables the tutoring to better match where the tutee needs help. Accordingly, allow student pairs to decide the assignment they do.
3. Tutors need structure to be effective. They should be trained on question prompt techniques that enable them to ask tutees to explain their thinking and ask for clarification. They should also be trained on how to correct misunderstandings.
4. Recommended frequency and duration is 2–3 times per week at 30 minutes per session. Greater frequency than this yields diminishing returns.

It is said that "to teach is to learn twice," a saying supported by the peer tutoring research. In terms of cost-benefit, peer tutoring is one of the few educational elements that provide both learning benefits and cost reductions. Relative to alternatives like decreasing class size or hiring additional teachers or professional tutors, peer tutoring is unmatched for its low cost, learning efficacy, and socioemotional benefits.

See also Classroom Management; Social-Emotional Learning; Teach-to-Learn

"Reciprocal Teaching: A Review of the Research" by Barak Rosenshine and Carla Meister, *Review of Educational Research*, 1994, 64(4), 479–530; "Preliminary Empirical Model of Crucial Determinants of Best Practice for Peer Tutoring on Academic Achievement" by K.C. Leung, *Journal of Educational Psychology*, 2015, 107(2), 558–579.

DO ···

- ◆ Do have tutor pairs work on teacher-provided assignments rather than discuss topics in the abstract.
- ◆ Do favor peer tutoring for low achieving and special needs students.
- ◆ Do give the peer tutor pair the agency to focus on areas of struggle they identify.
- ◆ Do ensure that tutors adequately understand what they are tutoring.
- ◆ Do encourage tutees to ask questions and articulate their confusions.
- ◆ Do limit tutoring programs to 30-minute sessions, 2–3 times/week.

DON'T ···

- ◆ Don't use peer tutors as a substitute for teachers.
- ◆ Don't only make top students tutors.
- ◆ Don't make tutors feel solely responsible for the other student's learning.
- ◆ Don't set up tutor pairs without structure and training.

REFLECT ···

Take the case of peer tutoring, where an older kid tutors a younger kid. This is really successful. The reason is it's a confluence of all these great social features. The kid is getting immediate feedback. He is having a chance to explain his or her reasoning to a peer. The peer is an older student, so they look up to them and kind of want to be around the older student. There's all these things that are conspiring for a very effective interaction, but you've got to get the social stuff right.

—Daniel Schwartz

"Strategies for Effective Teaching from Stanford's Dan Schwartz" by Lauren Faggella, *Summit Learning Blog*, December 8, 2017, https://blog.summitlearning.org/2017/12/dan-schwartz-podcast/.

32 Performance Load

The amount of effort required to complete an activity, which can either aid or inhibit learning.

People tend toward the paths of least resistance, whether it means taking escalators over stairs or using calculators over computation by hand. This creates special challenges for developing the mind and body, as the paths of least resistance rarely result in effective learning or fitness gains. This resistance can be conceptualized as a kind of performance load, and understanding and meting out the appropriate quantities and types of loads is fundamental to creating effective learning experiences.

Performance load refers to the total effort that is required to do something, both physical (kinematic) and mental (cognitive). Further, the performance load of an activity has elements that are intrinsic (essential to the activity) and extraneous (unrelated to the activity itself). Generally, intrinsic performance loads are good and extraneous performance loads are bad. For example, engaging students to solve goal-aligned problems within their capabilities would be intrinsic load, and everything else that required mental or physical effort—reading levels too difficult for the students, distractions from a noisy environment, time spent setting up and putting away equipment—would be an extraneous load. The goal of teachers is to proportion intrinsic cognitive loads to the abilities and skill levels of students, and to minimize extraneous cognitive and kinematic loads as much as possible.

Cognitive loads can exceed student abilities when the rate, quantity, and complexity of information presented are too great for students' working memories, when environments are distracting, and when students suffer impaired cognitive function due to stress or lack of sleep. The negative impact of overloading students can be dramatic. For example, compare two groups of students, one performing tasks with a low cognitive load and another with a high cognitive load. The high-cognitive-load group will make about five times more errors than the low-cognitive-load group.

This has clear implications for group activities. Groups can reduce the performance load of tasks by distributing the load among its members. However, if the intrinsic load is too distributed, learning will be ineffective and uneven among individual members. Further, if group governance is inefficient, the bureaucracy of the group interaction adds extraneous load to the task. The question is, at what group size is this tradeoff optimal for learning? The answer is likely two. In most contexts, dyads strike the best balance between productive intrinsic load sharing and minimal extraneous load due to group bureaucracy, outperforming both students working alone and larger group sizes.

See also Chunking; Classroom Design; Mnemonic Devices; Peer Tutoring

"Cognitive Load During Problem Solving: Effects on Learning" by John Sweller, *Cognitive Science*, 1988, 12(2), 257–285; "From Cognitive Load Theory to Collaborative Cognitive Load Theory" by Paul Kirschner et al., *International Journal of Computer-Supported Collaborative Learning*, 2018, 1–21.

✅ DO ···

- ◆ Do increase and decrease performance load according to student abilities.
- ◆ Do design presentations, worksheets, problem sets, and homework with working memory limits in mind.
- ◆ Do cut as much extraneous load (cognitive and kinematic) as possible.
- ◆ Do favor having clear roles for students working in groups.
- ◆ Do favor increased intrinsic performance load for learning, and decreased performance load for performance.
- ◆ Do favor dyads over larger groups.

❌ DON'T ···

- ◆ Don't assign tasks to groups without norms of communication, governance, or sufficient ability.
- ◆ Don't introduce group work when the task is not of sufficient complexity to warrant collaboration.
- ◆ Don't increase performance load just to increase the challenge.
- ◆ Don't present more information than necessary to complete the task.
- ◆ Don't "jazz up" presentations with irrelevant images or ornaments.

🕚 REFLECT ··

Working memory resources should be devoted to dealing with intrinsic cognitive load, not extraneous cognitive load. If extraneous cognitive load is reduced, more resources can be devoted to intrinsic information. Resources devoted to intrinsic information are germane which is positive.

—John Sweller

"An Interview with John Sweller" by Liberato Cardellini, *Education Policy, Management, and Quality*, 2015, 7(3), 127–134.

33 Personality

The ways in which people think, feel, and act that are roughly consistent across time and contexts.

Self-tests to determine our personality "type" abound and, while they might be entertaining, almost none of these are supported by evidence (e.g., Myers-Briggs). The exception is the Five-Factor Model, sometimes called the "Big Five," which has empirical support and important applications in the classroom. There are five factors of personality in this model, often referenced by the acronym OCEAN: Openness (informed, creative), Conscientiousness (organized, determined), Extraversion (sociable, self—confident), Agreeableness (accepting, cooperative), and Neuroticism (anxious, stressed). Some researchers have argued for a sixth factor, "Honesty-Humility," but the validity of this proposed addition is the subject of ongoing study.

Of these factors, conscientiousness reigns supreme when it comes to predicting academic achievement, career success, and long-term health. Conscientiousness refers to a person's ability to control their behavior and is strongly associated with inhibitory control, one of the three major executive functions. People who are conscientious tend to be more self-disciplined, deliberate in their actions, goal-oriented, and likely to follow rules and social norms. People who are not conscientious tend to be more undisciplined, impulsive, and non-conforming. Students ranking high in conscientiousness perform about a third of a letter grade better, on average, than their low-ranking peers. By way of comparison, this influence is above and beyond the influence of general intelligence.

Though similar, conscientiousness should not be confused with "grit." Grit is at best a sub-trait of conscientiousness and at worst just conscientiousness repackaged for popular consumption. The key difference centers on claims about malleability. Conscientiousness is a personality trait, which means it can evolve but is hard to change. Grit is proposed as a skill (or a malleable trait), which implies that it can be developed like any other skill. But there is little empirical support for grit as a construct distinct from conscientiousness, and little to no empirical support for the effectiveness of grit-based curricula. To the extent that grit exists, it is a small lever in a teacher toolbox of much larger levers.

Conscientiousness is not highly susceptible to intervention, but it can be developed with long-term practice of skills that promote conscientious habits in early childhood—e.g., practicing skills like goal setting, daily planning, arriving on time, maintaining an orderly environment at home and school, meeting commitments, and self-care and daily hygiene. There is also suggestive evidence that meditation emphasizing conscientious thinking may be an effective tool for developing conscientiousness minds.

See also Creativity; Executive Functions; Intelligence; Metacognition; Motivation

---

"Much Ado About Grit: A Meta-Analytic Synthesis of the Grit Literature" by Marcus Credé et al., *Journal of Personality and Social Psychology*, 2017, 113(3), 492–511; "A Meta-Analysis of the Five-Factor Model of Personality and Academic Performance" by Arthur Poropat, *Psychological Bulletin*, 2009, 135(2), 322–338.

DO ··

- Do recognize the role of conscientiousness as a predictor of academic achievement, career success, and long-term health.
- Do promote understanding of conscientious thinking and practice of conscientious behaviors, especially during early childhood through early adolescence.
- Do encourage persistence when student effort is directed toward well-defined and fixed goals.
- Do practice skills that reinforce self-regulation and self-control in early childhood.
- Do consider meditation exercises that emphasize conscientious themes.

 DON'T ··

- Don't use personality tests such as Myers-Briggs, etc., to classify students into personality "types."
- Don't encourage persistence in an approach when students need to change course or adopt new strategies to solve a problem.
- Don't adopt "grit" as a goal for students, label students as "gritty" or not, or expend resources toward grit-related educational programs.
- Don't punish students who productively challenge rules or expectations.

 REFLECT ··

Instead of focusing on lower-level traits, such as Grit, educational programs should aim to develop a broad set of Conscientiousness-related behaviors, as well as a rich repertoire of emotion-regulation strategies to address challenging school experiences.

—Zorana Ivcevic and Marc Brackett

"Predicting School Success: Comparing Conscientiousness, Grit, and Emotion Regulation Ability" by Zorana Ivcevic and Marc Brackett, *Journal of Research in Personality*, 2014, 52, 29–36.

34 Play

Enjoyable activities that aid social behavior, learning, and executive function.

Play as a pedagogy has long been a core tenet of early childhood education. Reggio Emilia, Waldorf, Montessori, Tools of the Mind, and Anji Play all consider play an essential part of how children learn, though they differ in the kinds of play, materials, social interaction, and the role of adults. Play generally benefits children, but those benefits are not universal across all ages and kinds of play. Play pedagogies can be roughly grouped into four types:

1. Faux Play: initiated and directed by the adult—essentially, direct instruction
2. Guided Play: initiated by the adult through materials or questions, but directed by the child's choices
3. Adult-Controlled Play: initiated by the child but directed by the adult
4. Free Play: initiated and directed by the child

Of the four types, guided play produces the best outcomes for young students. In this pedagogy, children play in environments that have been designed to afford certain kinds of learning opportunities and raise certain kinds of questions, like building with blocks, exploring buoyancy in water, or acting as a cashier. Asking children causal questions—e.g., why they think something happens as they play, or asking them to predict what would happen if they tried something new—aids their learning.

Play also appears effective at developing executive functions. At the end of kindergarten, children in play-based programs perform better on reading, executive control, and social interactions. However, by the end of elementary school, these benefits largely fade, with the exception of pro-social behaviors (social skill, role taking, resolving conflict, positive social activity, dealing with hierarchy and authority). And note that there is little evidence supporting the popular practice of pretend play—i.e., use of the imagination to create fantasy worlds or situations. Although this kind of play is fun for children and historically considered by psychologists as essential to healthy cognitive development, current research suggests no link between pretend play and creativity, intelligence, or problem solving. To the extent that there is a link, it, too, likely fades with time.

Play is a natural tendency observed in infants across the animal kingdom. It is, therefore, not surprising that pedagogies leveraging this tendency in humans can be effective. But not all types of play are effective at achieving targeted outcomes. It turns out that without design and adult guidance, play is not a pedagogy at all; it's just fun.

See also Intelligence; Executive Functions; Scaffolding; Student-Directed Learning

"Playing Around in School: Implications for Learning and Educational Policy" by Kelly Fisher et al., *The Oxford Handbook of the Development of Play* by A.D. Pellegrini (Ed.), 2011, Oxford University Press, 341–360; "The Impact of Pretend Play on Children's Development: A Review of the Evidence" by Angeline Lillard et al., *Psychological Bulletin*, January 2013, 139(1), 1–34. For a popular treatment, see *Montessori: The Science Behind the Genius* by Angeline Stoll Lillard, 2017, Oxford University Press.

DO ···

- ◆ Do favor guided play for young students—i.e., initiated by the teacher through materials or questions, but directed by the child's choices.
- ◆ Do set up the class environment to facilitate play with specific learning aims.
- ◆ Do encourage children to make plans for how they will act in given roles and scenarios.
- ◆ Do allow children to make their own decisions, but guide them through questions and co-play.
- ◆ Do provide opportunities for both individual and social play.

DON'T ···

- ◆ Don't require play to be pretend or imaginative.
- ◆ Don't remove children's choice from play.
- ◆ Don't punish children by restricting play.
- ◆ Don't use free play or faux play to facilitate academic learning in children under 7.

REFLECT ···

To let the child do as he likes when he has not yet developed any powers of control is to betray the idea of freedom.

—Maria Montessori

The *Absorbent Mind* by Maria Montessori, 1964, Theosophical Press.

35 Productive Failure

Designing activities that intentionally use failure to promote deeper learning.

Learning can occur through both success and failure. Supporting student success through scaffolding is generally preferable for straightforward skills. But when seeking to develop a deeper understanding of complex skills and systems, activities designed to have students productively fail are preferable. Further, the ability for students to deal with and learn from failure is essential for life, and an ability they cannot gain if always set up for success. The decision to design for productive failure depends on the kind of learning pursued, students' prior knowledge, and the number of possible approaches.

Productive failure is most effective for developing skills and deep understanding related to systems. Examples include modeling the climate impact of jet airplanes, calculating standard deviation from a data set, or even complex physical tasks like learning jiujitsu. These examples all have many component parts that are highly interrelated, lending themselves to a wide variety of creative approaches. Research suggests that when students attempt such things prior to receiving instruction, their resulting learning is around three times better than if first instructed. Mastering the skill itself does require successfully practicing the correct approach, so students' productive failures should be followed by the common tools of instruction, feedback, and relevant practice.

For failure to be productive, students need to have some relevant prior knowledge, though not so much that they are guaranteed success. By attempting activities beyond their abilities, students activate their prior knowledge and identify gaps between what they already know and what they need to know to be successful. This creates the proverbial teachable moment. Following failure when students are primed to receive instruction, teachers then highlight the differences between student attempts and possible correct approaches to enhance their understanding. Note that failure should be by design based on task difficulty and not due to unrelated obstacles, such as distractions.

Essential to productive failure is that students come up with many different possible solutions and approaches. The number of different ideas that students have is more important than whether or not they come up with the correct approach. By trying out different approaches, students are both activating a range of prior knowledge as well as discovering how the different facets of a skill or system interrelate. This not only creates a greater depth of understanding but also promotes creativity within the domain of study. Working in pairs or small groups can be an effective way to increase the variety of approaches generated. When a skill or concept is straightforward and doesn't lend itself to exploration, it is best to scaffold students' success.

See also   Discussion-Based Learning; Direct Instruction; Errors; Scaffolding

---

"Examining Productive Failure, Productive Success, Unproductive Failure, and Unproductive Success in Learning" by Manu Kapur, *Educational Psychologist*, 2016, 51(2), 289–299; "Learning From Failure: A Meta-Analysis of the Empirical Studies" by Aubteen Darabi et al., *Educational Technology Research and Development*, 2018, 1–18.

✅ DO

♦ Do use productive failure when students first learn complex systems or skills.

♦ Do favor having students work in small groups when generating multiple possible solutions.

♦ Do choose tasks that balance being engaging and challenging.

♦ Do provide students practice in applying the correct procedure after failing.

♦ Do design productive failure tasks where students have prior knowledge, but not enough to solve the problem.

♦ Do favor using productive failure for fostering transfer and deep conceptual understanding of systems.

♦ Do ensure that instruction contrasts students' approaches with the correct approach.

♦ Do favor productive failure on activities that are inherently motivating to students.

❌ DON'T

♦ Don't use productive failure when a skill or concept is straightforward.

♦ Don't just correct students after they fail—provide relevant coaching and practice.

♦ Don't have students attempt to solve a problem when they lack relevant pre-existing knowledge.

♦ Don't tell students correct information that is not linked to their failed attempts.

♦ Don't use productive failure when a skill or system lacks highly dependent parts or multiple approaches.

📝 REFLECT

The next time you are trying to learn something new, try not to take the easy way out. Try to figure it out yourself first, play with ideas, tinker a little, solve the problem on your own first, and in many ways as you possibly can. Focus not on the struggle, or any failure in not getting it right, but on how such an experience prepares you to learn from an expert later on. And that is what Productive Failure is all about: the art and science of intentionally designing for and bootstrapping failure for deep learning.

—Manu Kapur

"On the Other Side of Failure" by Manu Kapur, *GLOBE 1/2018 ETH Zurich*, January 2018, 37.

36 Progressive Disclosure

Modulating the difficulty and complexity of an experience based on students' expertise.

Progressive disclosure is a method of separating options and information into multiple layers, and then presenting those layers on a need-to-know basis to the student. The technique is primarily used to prevent cognitive overload and is commonly employed in game design, storytelling, instructional design, and the design of physical spaces. For example, a basic form of progressive disclosure occurs when a teacher covers up information on an overhead projector transparency and then progressively uncovers information on the transparency as the lecture proceeds. A more modern form is visible in many software interfaces, where advanced or infrequently used features are concealed from novice users. Novices operate in a basic environment until they are ready for additional functions, at which point advanced features are accessed and explored.

Learning efficiency benefits greatly from the use of progressive disclosure in this fashion. It is the basis for the spiral approach in education design, where initially just high-level facts are taught without details, and then the details are progressively layered in over time as learners progress. It is also related to the inverted pyramid method in journalism, in which information is progressively presented by order of importance, from most important to least important. Both of these approaches highlight a truism often not confronted by educators: Information presented to learners who are not interested or able to process it is effectively noise. And it can be demotivating. This is the reason theme park designers progressively disclose segments of their ride lines (sometimes augmented with entertainment) so that no one, in or out of the line, ever sees the depressing length of the line in its entirety. Information that is progressively disclosed to learners as they need or request it, or to learners who demonstrate readiness for it, is both better received and perceived as more relevant. Errors are reduced using this method, and, consequently, the amount of time and frustration spent recovering from errors is also reduced.

Progressive disclosure is an effective means of managing information complexity, but it is also an effective means of keeping learning experiences near the edge of learner ability. For example, in educational contexts, mastery and problem-based approaches present challenges to learners one at a time or in small sets and do not allow them to proceed to problems of greater difficulty until they demonstrate mastery of the problems at hand. This keeps the amount of information complexity low and the level of difficulty appropriate for the learner. Similarly, in game design, players are restricted to levels of game play until specific goals are achieved, at which point players "level up" and are allowed to proceed to more challenging levels. Whether in software design, curriculum design, or game design, the ability to simultaneously modulate the complexity and difficulty of learning experiences reveals the twofold power of progressive disclosure.

See also Chunking; Performance Load; Productive Failure; Reading Levels; Scaffolding

The Nurnberg Funnel: Designing Minimalist Instruction for Practical Computer Skill by John Carroll, 1990, MIT Press; "Training Wheels in a User Interface" by John Carroll and Caroline Carrithers, *Communications of the ACM*, 1984, 27(8), 800–806.

DO ···

- ◆ Do start with minimalist approaches, adding features, options, and details as learners progress or at their request.
- ◆ Do design curricula, lesson plans, and information presentations to accommodate students of varying levels of expertise.
- ◆ Do modulate the complexity of content, activities, and learning choices based on the expertise and abilities of students.
- ◆ Do conceal obscure or infrequently referenced information to all but advanced students.
- ◆ Do break up complex processes into discrete steps, letting students navigate them one step at a time.
- ◆ Do provide opportunities for learners to accelerate their learning—to test out of units, to read books above their grade level, or to do advanced extra-credit projects.

DON'T ···

- ◆ Don't overwhelm students with "everything at once."
- ◆ Don't reveal too much too quickly to novice learners, nor too little too slowly to advanced students.
- ◆ Don't be afraid to let students forge ahead and test the edge of their abilities.

REFLECT ···

Here's my best attempt to distill the operative rule behind progressive disclosure: Focus on essence. Elaborate on demand. In other words, begin by addressing fundamentals without cluttering detail. When more detail is needed, find the next appropriate state, and move there. Repeat as appropriate.

—Daniel Hardman

"Progressive Disclosure Everywhere" by Daniel Hardman, *Codecraft*, September 16, 2012, https://codecraft. co/2012/09/16/progressive-disclosure-everywhere/.

37 Project-Based Learning

Learning by creating artifacts that solve interesting or relevant problems.

Project-based learning has become increasingly popular in recent decades, with a variety of organizations offering their own definitions and best practices. Common to most of them is that project-based learning engages students in sustained pursuit of a problem, goal, or question that culminates in the creation of a well-developed artifact. The principal argument in favor of project-based learning is that it models the kinds of real-world challenges that most students will face in their professional lives—i.e., collaborating with peers on small teams, managing and navigating constraints, solving novel problems, iterating designs, and producing a high-quality deliverable—and therefore better transfers and prepares students for long-term success. Ironically, this is also the principal argument against project-based learning: It does not model the kinds of standardized assessments that are used to evaluate many students, teachers, and schools.

Much of the knowledge and skills acquired through collaborative, hands-on activities like project-based learning cannot effectively be measured using multiple-choice-like assessments—transfer limits apply to both learning and testing in dissimilar contexts. Yet the reality is that performance on standardized tests often determines education opportunity and access. Thus, educational programs incorporating project-based learning should also incorporate instruction that models the required assessments—i.e., standardized test taking. As repugnant as this will be to many educators, it is a practical consideration that serves the best interests of students. This is also important in understanding the state of the evidence: Much of the research on project-based learning has measured performance using standardized assessments, and correspondingly has yielded mixed results. While some studies show that project-based learning outperforms traditional instruction, just as many show the opposite. And meta-analyses that have basically summed these studies show mixed or weak results.

Two practices stand out in effective project-based learning: (1) projects have discrete stages tied to specific learning outcomes and (2) projects are "hard fun." Effective project-based learning breaks projects into logical chunks and uses these chunks to emphasize specific learning outcomes. Projects designed this way are roughly three times more effective than traditional approaches. Projects that are "hard fun" are both challenging and meaningful to students. In pursuing hard fun, students need to focus, overcome failure, and enjoy the challenge. Good storytelling can be essential in engaging students, turning dull technical challenges (like building a boat that could buoy 10 pounds) into hard fun (like building a boat to save dogs and cats during a flood). Neither pure fun nor a pure challenge works alone. Effective projects include both.

See also Depth of Processing; Direct Instruction; Student-Directed Learning; Transfer

---

"Motivating Project-Based Learning: Sustaining the Doing, Supporting the Learning" by Phyllis Blumenfeld et al., *Educational Psychologist*, 1991, 26(3–4), 369–398; "Beyond Breadth-Speed-Test: Toward Deeper Knowing and Engagement in an Advanced Placement Course" by Walter Parker et al., *American Educational Research Journal*, 2013, 50(6), 1424–1459.

DO ··

- ◆ Do break projects into stages that are tied to selected learning outcomes.
- ◆ Do make projects that are "hard fun"—i.e., both challenging and motivating.
- ◆ Do favor projects that allow students to work in ways that are particularly interesting or motivating to them.
- ◆ Do design projects that have goals and successes along the way to maintain motivation and provide opportunities for feedback.
- ◆ Do favor projects where students meaningfully collaborate.
- ◆ Do ensure that assessments match the way material is taught.
- ◆ Do favor projects where the final result is shared with an audience beyond the class.
- ◆ Do ensure students are well-practiced taking standardized assessments and tests.
- ◆ Do assess project-based learning using presentations, exhibitions, and studio critiques.

 **DON'T** ··

- ◆ Don't design projects without specific learning aims.
- ◆ Don't have beginner students make complex or ambiguous decisions.
- ◆ Don't micromanage or dictate students' activities step-by-step.
- ◆ Don't expect project-based learning to enhance performance on standardized tests.

REFLECT ··

Once I was alerted to the concept of "hard fun" I began listening for it and heard it over and over. It is expressed in many different ways, all of which all boil down to the conclusion that everyone likes hard challenging things to do. But they have to be the right things matched to the individual and to the culture of the times. These rapidly changing times challenge educators to find areas of work that are hard in the right way: they must connect with the kids and also with the areas of knowledge, skills and (don't let us forget) ethic, adults will need for the future world.

—Seymour Papert

"Hard Fun" by Seymour Papert, *Bangor Daily News*, June 24, 2002.

38 Reading Levels

A rating of text difficulty used to select texts for readers of different reading abilities.

Reading levels are ratings of text difficulty based on the complexity of words, grammar, sentences, and narrative structure. These ratings, typically reported as (or translated into) grade levels, are used to recommend, select, and sometimes even restrict texts for readers. For example, many teachers tailor reading lists to individual student reading levels, many school libraries limit access to books based on reading levels, and many schools advise parents to focus their child's at-home reading on texts within assessed reading levels. In this paradigm, reading levels are typically divided into three categories, labeled independent, instructional, and frustration. The independent level is relatively easy for readers (95 percent word accuracy). The instructional level is challenging but manageable for readers (90 percent word accuracy), and the frustration level is difficult for readers (less than 90 percent word accuracy). Teachers have traditionally been taught to give texts to students in which they can read words with about 90–95 percent accuracy—texts were to target a "Goldilocks zone" reading level: not too hard, not too easy, but just right.

The main problem with this paradigm is its complete lack of empirical support. The reading accuracy and comprehension goals are not derived from student performance, and the notion of matching levels is a guideline based on assumptions not evidence. Recent research suggests that students actually learn more when reading texts from a range of reading levels—both below and above a reader's rated ability—than when restricted to a narrow band. Texts below reading level develop confidence and fluency in reading, whereas texts above reading level result in greater growth than texts matched to reading levels. In fact, with the exception of kindergarten and first grade where decoding is the priority, the greatest reading growth comes not from reading texts at the instructional level, but at the frustration level. Clearly more difficult texts require more teacher and instructional support (e.g., partner reading, group discussions, audio- and video-texts), but the research is clear: from second grade on it is no pain, no gain.

Additionally, the effects of prior knowledge and inherent interest in a topic are as or more important than matching reading levels. Prior knowledge enables students to draw on their knowledge to fill in gaps in comprehension, and inherent interest gives them the motivation to push through when the reading gets tough. Prior knowledge and inherent interest not only enable students to explore texts beyond their grade level, these explorations increase vocabulary and familiarity with more complex grammar and sentence structures. In fact, the role of prior knowledge is so important in the development of general reading comprehension that texts in history, science, mathematics, literature, and the arts should form the backbone of all 2–12 curricula.

See also   Deliberate Practice; Dual Coding; Motivation; Performance Load; Transfer

"The Effects of Dyad Reading and Text Difficulty on Third-Graders' Reading Achievement" by Lisa Trottier Brown et al., *Journal of Educational Research*, 2017, doi:10.1080/00220671.2017.1310711; "Reconstructing Readability: Recent Developments and Recommendations in the Analysis of Text Difficulty" by Rebekah Benjamin, *Educational Psychology Review*, 2012, 24(1), 63–88.

DO ···

- ◆ Do treat reading levels as rough guidelines only.
- ◆ Do let passion, curiosity, and prior knowledge drive text selection more than grade or reading levels.
- ◆ Do have students read across subjects to develop broad prior knowledge.
- ◆ Do encourage students to read texts below and above their grade levels, providing appropriate levels of instructional support for difficult texts.
- ◆ Do promote access to texts—at home, on buses, over summers, etc.
- ◆ Do provide increased support to students reading at a frustration level.
- ◆ Do encourage students to read widely and extensively.

 DON'T ···

- ◆ Don't use reading levels to restrict or limit access to texts.
- ◆ Don't use student frustration to justify reducing text difficulty.
- ◆ Don't allow students who struggle with reading to read less.
- ◆ Don't focus elementary programs on math and reading at the expense of other subjects like history and science—promote reading in all disciplines.

 REFLECT ···

For generations, reading experts have told teachers that they had to teach students to read at their instructional levels. Teachers were admonished that if they taught children with books that were too easy, there would be nothing for the kids to learn. . . . Unfortunately, this insightful plan (that many of us have used in our classrooms) was just made up. In today's parlance, the instructional level is "fake news." No one bothered to do studies to determine whether that kind of book matching was beneficial to kids or not!

—Timothy Shanahan

"New Evidence on Teaching Reading at Frustration Levels" by Timothy Shanahan, *Shanahan on Literacy*, May 14, 2017, https://shanahanonliteracy.com.

39 Retrieval Practice

Practicing the retrieval and reconstruction of knowledge to promote long-term retention.

What is the best way to learn? It's not traditional instruction. It's not intensive review sessions. And it's not self-directed study. Simply stated, it's taking tests. Or, more accurately, retrieving and reconstructing knowledge as one does with tests, flashcards, quizzes, or Q&A sessions. The learning gains from such activities are commonly referred to as the "testing effect." Traditional educational approaches emphasize input or storage processes—i.e., pushing information into long-term memory—such as rereading material, reviewing notes, and relistening to a lecture. These approaches pale in comparison and effectiveness to approaches that emphasize output or retrieval—i.e., pulling information out from long-term memory—such as tests of various kinds.

Why is practicing retrieval more effective than practicing storage? When students retrieve knowledge, two things happen that benefit long-term retention. First, they discover what they know and don't know. It's easy for students to think they understand a text they have read, but having to answer questions about the text literally puts their knowledge to the test. Second, the act of recalling information itself roots it in long-term memory by strengthening the connections and pathways between a given context and the relevant knowledge. Neither of these events occurs as effectively in storage practice.

For these reasons, retrieval practice generally outperforms all traditional forms of studying. For example, take a middle-ranked student from a class of 100 students using traditional studying techniques. Give this student practice tests instead of studying and research suggests their class ranking would improve by about 23 students. And the gains are better when there is feedback. Pre-tests are similarly effective. Students who are first tested, then presented with the correct information, remember on average 10 percent more than those who are either presented with the same information twice or tested and then get delayed feedback.

But not all tests are created equal. The most superficial type of retrieval practice emphasizes rote retrieval of facts, which is basically only useful for exam preparation. In rote retrieval, the retrieval practice closely resembles the final assessment in content and format (e.g., multiple-choice, short answer, and essay questions). By contrast, rich retrieval builds knowledge and skills by using tests to prepare students to synthesize and apply their learning in novel contexts. In rich retrieval, the retrieval practice uses open-ended questions or practical applications that change as the student improves. There is no learning strategy more effective than retrieval practice, both for building factual knowledge through rote retrieval and for developing expertise through rich retrieval.

See also   Assessment, Self; Deliberate Practice; Feedback; Interleaving; Spacing

"The Critical Role of Retrieval Practice in Long-Term Retention" by Henry Roediger III and Andrew Butler *Trends in Cognitive Sciences*, 2011, 15(1), 20–27; "Learning Versus Performance: An Integrative Review" by Nicholas Soderstrom and Robert Bjork, *Perspectives on Psychological Science*, 2015, 10(2), 176–199.

✔ DO

- Do provide periodic no-stakes quizzes for the most important material.
- Do have students study through retrieval practice (e.g., flashcards, practice questions) instead of review.
- Do favor open-ended retrieval practice (e.g., short answer, essay) over closed questions (e.g., multiple choice).
- Do encourage students to develop their own questions to test their knowledge.
- Do test students on the most important concepts before the material is introduced.
- Do encourage students to test themselves on concepts they think they already know.
- Do discourage students from rereading material.

✖ DON'T

- Don't have students passively review important information multiple times.
- Don't use tests only as knowledge assessments or to assign scores.
- Don't test important information only once.
- Don't test immediately after material is learned—allow a delay.
- Don't only use rote retrieval—rich retrieval is essential for developing mastery.

❝ REFLECT

Retrieval practice—recalling facts or concepts or events from memory—is a more effective learning strategy than review by rereading. Flashcards are a simple example. Retrieval strengthens the memory and interrupts forgetting. A single, simple quiz after reading a text or hearing a lecture produces better learning and remembering than rereading the text or reviewing lecture notes.

—Peter Brown

Make It Stick: The Science of Successful Learning by Peter Brown et al., 2014, Belknap Press.

40 Scaffolding

Providing the minimum academic support required for students to achieve success.

In the construction of buildings, scaffolding is used to support structures until they are strong enough to stand on their own. This idea is intended to apply similarly in education, where scaffolding instruction means supporting students until they can independently and successfully perform a specific task. The colloquial use of the term scaffolding has unfortunately become synonymous with most assistance students receive, whether feedback, a diagram, or coaching. While it can take many forms, scaffolding amounts to providing the minimum amount of new information required to prevent failure.

Constraining new information is necessary for all unfamiliar material or introductory learning, whether conceptual or skills-based. Limiting new learning to around four or five items maximizes the probability students will understand a concept or perform a task with relative ease. Common tactics for limiting the quantity of new learning include adjusting the unsolved steps in a worked example, focusing students on one aspect of a problem to be solved, or interspersing short instructional sections with practice. By closely monitoring student performance, teachers can identify what has become familiar and maintain introducing four to five new items with minimal failure. In the construction metaphor, scaffolding is removed once the building is done. In learning, similarly, scaffolding is systematically reduced as students demonstrate increasing competency.

A common misunderstanding of scaffolding is that prerequisite knowledge, skills, or cognitive stages exist that students must obtain before they can learn new material. While such linearity is tempting, it largely lacks empirical support. Most learning—whether math, science, writing, or reading—does not follow a linear path with clear dependencies, but rather has sets of related skills or concepts. Similarly, students do not progress through clear-cut and pervasive cognitive stages. Rather than basing scaffolding on purported sequences of knowledge or developmental stages, it should be adjusted based on student performance.

For learning that is not introductory, scaffolding is necessary in cases where failure could be dangerous or unproductive—i.e., when it poses risks to life or property, when the result is demotivating, or when it is unlikely to be a productive experience. Be careful not to over-scaffold, as struggle is a necessary part of learning. For advanced students, scaffolding can actually impair learning, a phenomenon known as the expertise reversal effect. In this way, scaffolding and productive failure sit at opposite ends of the same instructional continuum: Scaffolding is more effective for beginning students and simple topics, and productive failure is more effective for advanced students and complex topics.

See also Feedback; Productive Failure; Progressive Disclosure; Reading Levels

"Scaffolding in Teacher–Student Interaction: A Decade of Research" by Janneke Van de Pol et al., *Educational Psychology Review*, 2010, 22(3), 271–296; "Effectiveness of Computer-Based Scaffolding in the Context of Problem-Based Learning for STEM Education: Bayesian Meta-Analysis" by Nam Ju Kim et al., *Educational Psychology Review*, 2018, 30(2), 397–429.

DO ··

- ◆ Do provide the minimum amount of academic support to prevent failure.
- ◆ Do scaffold all new and introductory learning.
- ◆ Do scaffold by providing worked-out solutions, practice exercises, and self-assessments.
- ◆ Do favor either adjusting the amount of new information based on student performance or having students select the desired level of challenge.
- ◆ Do limit new learning to four or five items to minimize failure.
- ◆ Do reduce scaffolding as student competence increases.

 DON'T ··

- ◆ Don't use scaffolding when students are advanced in a subject area.
- ◆ Don't scaffold according to pre-set sequences of knowledge or cognitive stages.
- ◆ Don't always increase new information over time but increase or decrease based on student performance.
- ◆ Don't simplify activities so much that they become uninteresting.
- ◆ Don't model an example when students already have a good understanding.

 REFLECT ··

Instructors and students need to appreciate the distinction between learning and performance and understand that expediting acquisition performance today does not necessarily translate into the type of learning that will be evident tomorrow. On the contrary, conditions that slow or induce more errors during instruction often lead to better long-term learning outcomes, and thus instructors and students, however disinclined to do so, should consider abandoning the path of least resistance with respect to their own teaching and study strategies. After all, educational interventions should be based on evidence, not on historical use or intuition.

—Nicholas Soderstrom and Robert Bjork

"Learning Versus Performance: An Integrative Review" by Nicholas Soderstrom and Robert Bjork, *Perspectives on Psychological Science*, 2015, 10(2), 176–199.

41 Serial Position Effects

Items at the beginning and end of a list are more easily recalled than items in the middle.

Serial position effects occur when people try to recall items from a list or serial presentation. In such cases, items at the beginning and end are better recalled than the items in the middle. For example, when learning lists of things such as the alphabet, math tables, U.S. presidents, or a long poem or song, the information at the beginning and end are more easily recalled than the information in the middle. Additionally, when learning information in a serial form, items tend to be recalled in the same serial order, with each item in the sequence acting as a memory cue for the next. For example, when recalling a middle letter position in the alphabet, people generally have to recite a large part of the alphabet to determine it. The improved recall for items at the beginning of a list is called a primacy effect. The improved recall for items at the end of a list is called a recency effect. The improved recall of items together in a sequence is called a contiguity effect. Serial position effects are observed across all ages, cultures, and even in other primates such as chimpanzees.

Primacy effects occur because the initial items in a list are stored in long-term memory more efficiently than items later in the list. Recency effects occur because the last few items in a list are still in working memory and readily available for a brief time. Contiguity effects occur because items that are presented closely together in time and space become associated with one another in memory. For typical lists and classroom presentations, items presented early have the greatest influence; they are not only better recalled for longer periods of time, but they also influence the interpretation of later items. For auditory presentations, the last items in the presentation have the greatest influence. In all cases, serial items tend to be recalled in the order they are learned.

The practical implications for teachers are clear: New and essential information should be presented at the beginning of instructional sessions, reinforced at the end of instructional sessions, with activities to explore and practice sandwiched in between. If flexibility of recall is desired—i.e., the ability to recall particular items independent of contiguous items in the list—then items should not be learned in a serial fashion. In decision-making and persuasion contexts, when multiple presentations occur one right after the other and the selection decision must be made soon after the last presentation (for example, judging a talent show or selecting a science fair winner), the recency effect has the greatest influence on the decision. If the selection decision happens a day or more after the last presentation, the primacy effect will have the greatest influence. This is related to a selection bias known as order effects—first and last items in a list are more likely to be selected than items in the middle (e.g., the order of candidates on a ballot).

See also Choice Overload; Chunking; Dual Coding; Mnemonic Devices

"Three More Semantic Serial Position Functions and a SIMPLE Explanation" by Matthew Kelley et al., *Memory & Cognition*, 41, 600–610; "First Guys Finish First: The Effects of Ballot Position on Election Outcomes" by Jennifer Steen and Jonathan GS Koppell, *Presentation at the 2001 Annual Meeting of the American Political Science Association*, San Francisco.

✓ DO

- Do favor presenting new and essential information at the beginning of learning experiences and materials, including worksheets, lectures, activities, lessons, etc.
- Do favor reviewing new and essential information at the end of learning experiences and materials.
- Do favor using the middle of learning experiences and materials for noncritical information or dedicate additional time to practice middle items as they are less easily recalled.
- Do have students practice recalling the full series when emphasis is on learning the full list (e.g., ABCs), and practice recall of individual items when emphasis is on learning items independent of the list (e.g., planets of the solar system).
- Do consider order effects when designing ballots and other selection systems, favoring randomly ordered sequences over fixed-ordered sequences to neutralize the bias.

✗ DON'T

- Don't present essential information in the middle of learning experiences and materials.
- Don't teach information in serial form when flexibility of item recall is desired.
- Don't rely on serial positions in lieu of creating engaging, interesting content—interesting content oft repeated is more memorable than dull content at the beginning or end of a lecture.

❝ REFLECT

Even with the best of intentions, teachers with little knowledge of the primacy-recency effect can do the following: After getting focus by telling the class the day's lesson objective, the teacher takes attendance, distributes the previous day's homework, collects that day's homework, requests notes from students who were absent, and reads an announcement about a club meeting after school. . . . As a finale, the teacher tells the students that they were so well-behaved during the lesson that they can do anything they want during the last five minutes of class as long as they are quiet. I have observed this scenario, and I can attest that the next day those students remembered who was absent and why, which club met after school, and what they did at the end of the period.

—David Sousa

How the Brain Learns (5th ed.) by David Sousa, 2017, Sage Publications.

42 Sleep Strategies

Techniques to ensure quality sleep so as to promote memory formation and overall cognitive functioning.

Across ages, cultures, subjects, and teachers, the most universally impactful variable on learning happens at home and at night: sleep. Sufficient quality sleep is essential to academic success. The average timing and duration of sleep is a function of circadian rhythm, which changes with age. Babies and young children tend to favor mornings but shift to favoring nights in the teenage years. This shift is called sleep phase delay. The table that follows lists average sleep requirements for different age groups. While the averages do not apply to everyone, in general, sleep rhythms inconsistent with these durations and times will result in sleep deficit and diminished cognitive function results. Note that sleeping significantly more or less than these durations (i.e., sleeping too much or too little) can both impair cognitive function.

AGE (years)	DURATION (hours)	AVERAGE WAKEUP and SLEEP TIMES
3–5	11.5	7:00 am–7:30 pm
6–13	10	7:30 am–9:30 pm
14–17	9	8:45 am–11:30 pm
18–25	8	8:30 am–12:30 pm
26–64	8	7:30 am–11:30 pm
64+	7.5	6:45 am–12:15 pm

Synchronizing the start of school with circadian rhythms is one of the best ways to ensure that students get adequate sleep and enable effective learning. The group most negatively impacted by most school schedules is teenagers. When school start times for this group are delayed until 9:30 am, the benefit is equivalent to replacing a highly ineffective teacher with a highly effective teacher. Note that the benefit of later start times does not extend to students below eighth grade.

Teachers can also promote strategies for quality sleep with students and parents, such as (1) maintain a consistent sleep schedule, even on weekends; (2) don't eat within two hours of bedtime; (3) avoid caffeine before bedtime; (4) create a dark, quiet sleeping environment; (5) do not exercise before bedtime; (6) avoid snoozing the alarm since it actually increases drowsiness; and (7) avoid blue light from phones, televisions, and LED clocks a minimum of two hours before bedtime.

See also Classroom Management; Exercise Effects; Metacognition; Parent Engagement

"Effects of Sleep Manipulation on Cognitive Functioning of Adolescents: A Systematic Review" by Eduard de Bruin et al., *Sleep Medicine Reviews*, 2017, 32, 45–57; "Rise and Shine: The Effect of School Start Times on Academic Performance from Childhood Through Puberty" by Jennifer Heissel and Samuel Norris, *Journal of Human Resources*, 2017, 0815–7346R1. For a popular treatment, see "Are Sleepy Students Learning?" by Daniel Willingham, *American Educator*, 2013, 36(4), 35–39.

DO ···

- ◆ Do favor later school start times when possible, especially for teenage students.
- ◆ Do encourage students to go to bed and wake up at the same time every day of the week.
- ◆ Do encourage students to maximize exposure to natural light after waking up.
- ◆ Do encourage students to exercise during the day to fall asleep more easily.
- ◆ Do educate students and parents of the recommended sleep duration and times.
- ◆ Do encourage students to gradually make their bedtimes earlier as a way to get more sleep.
- ◆ Do teach students about the importance and benefits of sleep.
- ◆ Do introduce students to apps that filter blue light on their electronic devices.

DON'T ···

- ◆ Don't have students exposed to or using electronic devices before going to sleep.
- ◆ Don't support students in getting a few more minutes of sleep by snoozing their alarms.
- ◆ Don't encourage students to maximize sleep at the expense of a consistent sleep schedule.
- ◆ Don't compromise learning for scheduling or logistical convenience.

REFLECT ···

If you knew that in your child's school there was a toxic substance that reduced the capacity to learn, increased the chances of a car crash and made it likely that 20 years from now he would be obese and suffer from hypertension, you'd do everything possible to get rid of that substance and not worry about cost. Early start times are toxic.

—Judith Owens

"Resetting the Clock: High School Start Times" by Karen Clarkson, *Washington Parent*, April 1, 2013.

43 Social-Emotional Learning

The ability and skill to relate to others, set goals, manage emotions, and resolve conflict.

Beyond academic achievement, it is crucial for students to be emotionally healthy, avoid risky behavior, be caring and empathic, come to reasoned judgments about the right actions when values are at odds, and take action to solve local and global problems. Social-emotional learning (SEL) is valuable inherently, but it also increases academic achievement. Research suggests that taking a middle-ranked student in a class of 100 students without SEL instruction and placing this student in a class with an effective SEL program would increase that student's academic rank by approximately 11 students.

The academic gains are likely attributable to improvements in the ability to self-regulate, which is the ability to control and manage thoughts, feelings, and behaviors. Such students become more self-aware and confident in their abilities, as well as develop the mettle to persist in the face of challenges. Additionally, students with developed social-emotional abilities set higher academic goals, have greater self-discipline, and are better able to organize and plan their learning activities to achieve academic goals. One study analyzed the long-term economic impact of SEL programs and found that every dollar invested yielded $11 in returns by reducing crime, increasing lifetime earnings, and promoting better mental and physical health.

The best way to develop social and emotional skills is through a combination of everyday reinforcement, for example through classroom norms and rituals, and direct instruction. We have quick, intuitive reactions to situations and interactions, and such social-emotional reactions are best coached in real time and in real contexts. But we also need to acquire basic social-emotional knowledge and skills, which are best learned like any other set of skills. The most effective approaches to SEL combine these processes, infusing SEL in everyday life and teaching skills explicitly.

Cognitive and emotional processes help develop social and emotional skills. Classroom expectations are more effective when students are involved in creating them. Discussion of dilemmas is more likely to be effective when it includes consideration of what the student would do or how someone the student knows might feel. Active strategies, such as projects involving volunteering, perspective taking, root-cause analysis, and long-term planning are all effective methods to increase SEL. The good news is that social and emotional skills can be developed. Teachers should therefore not only focus on academic skills but also on the social-emotional skills needed to develop healthy, well-rounded, and caring students able to engage and solve local and global problems.

See also   Classroom Management; Motivation; Personality; Student-Teacher Relationship

"The Impact of Enhancing Students' Social and Emotional Learning: A Meta-Analysis of School-Based Universal Interventions" by Joseph Durlak et al., *Child Development*, 2011, 82(1), 405–432; "Social and Emotional Learning in Schools: From Programs to Strategies and Commentaries" by Stephanie Jones and Suzanne Bouffard, *Social Policy Report*, 2012, 26(4), 1–33; "The Economic Value of Social and Emotional Learning" by Clive Belfield et al., *Center for Benefit-Cost Studies in Education*, 2015.

DO ··

- ◆ Do adopt an evidence-based SEL program and pursue a systemic approach to planning and implementation.
- ◆ Do combine everyday reinforcement and direct instruction to develop SEL, ensuring that adults in the school practice the social-emotional skills that they preach.
- ◆ Do encourage students to express and reason about their social and emotional challenges.
- ◆ Do provide opportunities to practice taking multiple perspectives, including first-, second-, and third-person perspectives.
- ◆ Do engage students in projects that support them to identify the root causes of problems and take wide-ranging actions to address them.
- ◆ Do encourage students to volunteer and experience learning in the service of causes greater than themselves.
- ◆ Do partner with parents and community organizations to extend SEL programs.

❌ DON'T ··

- ◆ Don't institute SEL programs in isolated classes or meetings without integrating skill development into the everyday classroom and school-wide experiences.
- ◆ Don't rely only on direct instruction to develop social and emotional competence.
- ◆ Don't ignore spaces like hallways, playgrounds, and cafeterias to learn and practice social-emotional skills.
- ◆ Don't focus exclusively on personal responsibility, rule following, and compliance.

REFLECT ··

To the extent that we strengthen SEL, we increase that likelihood that students will learn to the best of their ability. After decades of practice, we know that social and emotional skills and values can indeed be taught. We know that when taught and modeled well by adults in schools, bonding increases, problem behaviors decrease, and test scores go up . . .

To the extent that we ignore SEL, we increase the likelihood that students will further disengage from learning, and that teachers will become increasingly frustrated by the ways in which the system makes it difficult for them to teach.

—Timothy Shriver and Jennifer Buffett

Handbook of Social and Emotional Learning: Research and Practice by Timothy Shriver and Jennifer Buffett, 2015, The Guilford Press.

44 Spacing

Breaking practice into small sessions with delays in between to increase long-term retention.

Given the option of practicing one type of activity in one long session (known as massing) or practicing this activity in multiple, shorter sessions spaced out over time (known as spacing), the latter results in better long-term learning. For example, students who cram for five hours on the night before an exam may do well on the test, but they will forget what they've learned shortly thereafter. By contrast, students who study for one hour per night for five days will perform as well on the exam and retain what they've learned for a much longer period. The retention benefits are significant: Research suggests that a group learning using spaced practice will remember about 67 percent better than a group learning the same material through massed practice.

So what is the optimal spacing for practice sessions? It depends on the target retention interval—i.e., how long you want students to remember. For retention intervals of less than six months, the spacing gaps should be 20 percent of the total retention interval. That means that for a recall date in one week, practice should be spaced every one to two days; for a test in one month, it should be every six days. For retention intervals greater than six months, the spacing gaps should be 10 percent of the total retention interval. So to prepare for an exam in one year, the spacing would be set at one practice session per month.

It is important to note that spacing occurs at the level of a specific item, not at the subject level. This means that a particular fact (e.g., the causes of WW1) or skill (e.g., solving an equation for two variables) should be spaced out, not history or math class itself. And spacing practice does not mean simply reviewing the same material repeatedly. Practice sessions are only effective when they require practicing recall of content or practicing a skill. For example, giving a review lecture will be less effective than giving a practice test, giving homework that includes problems from the current unit will be less effective than homework that includes items from previous units, and giving a final exam that covers only recently taught material will be less effective than giving a final that covers all previously taught material.

Spacing is a powerful tool for educators, but not everything needs to be remembered long-term. It is important to weigh the administrative and planning costs of spacing practice against its learning benefits, and this typically means using spaced practice on the most important material only: key concepts, foundational skills, and so on. While the possible applications of spaced practice could apply to all content—historical facts, basketball, factoring—the key to successful use is prioritizing the essential learning goals and focusing practice accordingly.

See also Depth of Processing; Homework; Interleaving; Retrieval Practice; Study Tactics

"Learning Versus Performance: An Integrative Review" by Nicholas Soderstrom and Robert Bjork, *Perspectives on Psychological Science*, 2015, 10(2), 176–199. For a popular treatment, see *Make It Stick: The Science of Successful Learning* by Peter Brown et al., 2014, Belknap Press.

DO ···

- ◆ Do plan spaced practice opportunities for the most important material.
- ◆ Do space practice activities at approximately 20 percent of the recall date for less than six months and at approximately 10 percent for more than six months.
- ◆ Do separate instruction into small sections to avoid massed practice.
- ◆ Do integrate previously learned material into the current unit.
- ◆ Do teach students about the benefits of spacing versus cramming.
- ◆ Do encourage students to review key topics they may feel they already know.

 DON'T ···

- ◆ Don't review material immediately after teaching.
- ◆ Don't cease all practicing important topics even when students practice with ease.
- ◆ Don't only review material through instruction but also engage students in practice.
- ◆ Don't have students practice a topic multiple times in a single session.
- ◆ Don't space everything, only what is most important.

REFLECT ···

The more [practice sessions] are massed together, the more you will see apparent benefits in the short term. The more they are spread apart, the more you'll see real benefits in the long-term.

—Robert Bjork

"Spacing Improves Long-Term Retention" [video interview], *UCLA Bjork Learning and Forgetting Lab*, https://bjorklab.psych.ucla.edu/research/.

45 Student-Directed Learning

Allowing students to learn with minimal guidance to improve learning and transfer.

Giving students significant control over their learning is increasingly popular and is foundational to pedagogies such as project-based learning, problem-based learning, and inquiry learning. Common to these approaches is the belief that students, not teachers, should determine and largely drive the key aspects of the learning experience. So should students direct their own learning? The short answer: sometimes.

In general, students learn best when teachers design the resources, orchestrate the activities, and provide feedback on performance—i.e., students learn best when teachers direct the learning. For example, give two groups of students the same set of novel, complex problems, one with instruction and one without, and the group receiving instruction will consistently outperform the student-directed group. Similarly, when students are presented with novel problems, roughly half of what they spend their time on tends to be irrelevant to actually solving the problem. But there are three conditions when student-directed learning is more effective than teacher-directed: (1) students possess advanced knowledge or general ability, (2) students are deconstructing solutions, and (3) students are learning a procedural skill that is too complex to be taught in advance and remembered.

When students have advanced knowledge or general ability, teacher-directed learning can actually be detrimental. For example, take a class of students who are deeply familiar with a text. Teacher-directed learning on this text can actually have negative learning consequences, a phenomenon known as the expertise reversal effect. When students have advanced knowledge of content, student-directed learning is preferred. The same is true when students are engaged in deconstructing, hacking, or reverse engineering objects, solutions, or phenomena, or when deriving rules or patterns from examples or data. When these activities are paired with teach-to-learn and discussion pedagogies, the result is better retention and transfer than with teacher-directed study.

Lastly, when introducing a new skill requiring more than five unfamiliar steps, teacher-directed approaches are less effective than hands-on practice with feedback. In such cases, keeping the unfamiliar steps in mind causes cognitive overload, and therefore it is better to go straight to practice. For example, imagine teaching a student how to ride a bike for the first time. It is more effective to get them on the bike and provide real-time feedback than to first load them up with verbal instructions. While students should generally not direct their own learning, there are times when it is the tool of choice. The key is knowing when and then using the right tool for the job.

See also   Direct Instruction; Play; Scaffolding; Teach-to-Learn; Productive Failure

---

"When Is PBL More Effective? A Meta-Synthesis of Meta-Analyses Comparing PBL to Conventional Classrooms" by Johannes Strobel and Angela Van Barneveld, *Interdisciplinary Journal of Problem-Based Learning*, 2009, 3(1), 4; "Does Discovery-Based Instruction Enhance Learning?" by Louis Alfieri et al., *Journal of Educational Psychology*, 2011, 103(1), 1.

DO

- ◆ Do let students direct their learning when they have advanced knowledge or skill in a domain.
- ◆ Do design activities that require students to deconstruct, hack, or reverse engineer objects, solutions, and phenomena.
- ◆ Do encourage teach-to-learn and discussion when employing student-directed learning.
- ◆ Do engage students to independently generate explanations, rules, and models based on data and examples.
- ◆ Do have students try out complex new skills with just-in-time feedback before providing instruction.
- ◆ Do adapt feedback and practice strategies based on student skill levels and pedagogy.

✖ DON'T

- ◆ Don't rely on just one pedagogy or approach for all students and learning contexts.
- ◆ Don't let students direct their own learning unless they are advanced, or unless the environment and activities have been specifically designed to practice independent skills.
- ◆ Don't make students choose how to learn new content.
- ◆ Don't provide extensive instruction before introducing new complex skills.
- ◆ Don't abandon direct instruction.

❝ REFLECT

[The] ideal learning environments for experts and novices differ because experts and novices differ. While experts often thrive without much guidance, nearly everyone else thrives when provided direct instructional support and guidance.

—Paul Kirschner

"Inquiry Learning Isn't—A Call for Direct Explicit Instruction" by Paul Kirschner, *ResearchED*, 2018, 1(1).

46 Student-Teacher Relationship

Bonds between students and teachers that support student achievement.

Positive student-teacher relationships lead to higher student motivation, engagement, and academic achievement, prevent alienation, and decrease disruption. For example, take a middle-ranked student from a class of 100 students without strong student-teacher relationships. Place that student with a teacher with whom they have a strong relationship and research suggests their class ranking would improve by about 26 students. This is true for students of all ages, genders, and backgrounds, but particularly true for students of lower socio-economic status where there is a greater risk of academic failure. The key attributes of teachers who develop positive student-teacher relationships are warmth, empathy, and high expectations. To best develop this profile:

- Observe students and class activities, listen, understand student perspectives, communicate this understanding, and take compassionate action;
- Get to know students personally—their experiences, interests, and challenges, and how their cultures and family contexts differ; and
- Act as a mentor focused on student success. Teachers as mentors should have high academic expectations, inspire confidence on the part of students, and work closely with students to reach them. An effective way to build positive relationships is to identify common goals and then actively partner with students and families to achieve them. Note that teacher-as-mentor is not the same as teacher-as-friend. Teachers should prioritize student achievement and success over popularity.

The impact of negative, conflict-ridden student-teacher relationships is more pronounced and long-lasting with younger students, and the impact of positive student-teacher relationships is more pronounced with older, adolescent students—this despite the fact that teachers tend to spend less time during the school day with older students.

The social-emotional competence of teachers is also important in developing relationships with students. Their self-awareness and ability to self-regulate, their attentiveness and responsiveness to the needs of others, their ability to foster positive relationships with students, parents, and other adults all serve as models for students.

When building positive relationships with students, less is more. The goal should be to build relationships that are strong enough to allow self-sufficiency and self-determination on the part of students as they engage in learning. Effective classroom management and the development of social and emotional learning among students also support positive student-teacher relationship development. These efforts go hand in hand.

See also Classroom Management; Engagement, Student; Social-Emotional Learning

"Learner-Centered Teacher-Student Relationships Are Effective: A Meta-Analysis" by Jeffrey Cornelius-White, *Review of Educational Research*, 2007, 77(1), 113–143; "The Influence of Affective Teacher–Student Relationships on Students' School Engagement and Achievement: A Meta-Analytic Approach" by Debora Roorda et al., *Review of Educational Research*, 2011, 81(4), 493–529.

DO ··

- Do assume the mentor role with students, partnering with them to reach their learning goals and holding high expectations.
- Do get to know your students, including their interests and challenges.
- Do allow students to get to know you by sharing some of your interests and personal experiences with them.
- Do foster empathy for students by seeking to understand their perspectives.
- Do respond to the emotions of students with caring attention.
- Do model the healthy expression of your own emotion.
- Do pay attention to your own physical and emotional health and take steps to avoid burnout.
- Do ensure follow through on commitments to students.
- Do enforce the classroom management strategy fairly and objectively.

DON'T ··

- Don't confuse mentorship with friendship or popularity.
- Don't confuse warm relationships with a well-managed classroom.
- Don't treat some students more warmly than others.
- Don't limit feedback or assignments in order to be liked by students.
- Don't rely on coercive and punitive tactics to achieve behavior change.
- Don't ignore signs of burnout—it will compromise relationships with students.

REFLECT ··

One of the most interesting aspects of powerful teacher-student relationships is that they are forged by behavior and words as opposed to thoughts and feelings. Stated differently, it is not what a teacher thinks and feels about a particular student that forges a positive relationship with the student. Rather, it is how the teacher speaks to and behaves with the student that communicates respect and acceptance.

—Robert Marzano

The Highly Engaged Classroom by Robert Marzano and Debra Pickering, 2010, Marzano Research.

47 Study Tactics
Strategies used to improve and maintain understanding.

Whether preparing for a test or completing an assignment, the tactics that students employ learning on their own largely determine their academic success. In general, the effectiveness of study tactics is linked to the extent to which they require students to think deeply about content. Study tactics can be broadly grouped into four categories, listed by order of effectiveness: retrieval, planning, recording, and text marking.

Retrieval tactics are hands-down the most effective methods of study for achieving long-term learning across all subjects, grades, and ability levels. They include practicing the recall of content using flashcards, practice questions, self-quizzing, or verbal Q&A. For example, take a middle-ranked student from a class of 100 students. If that student were to begin self-quizzing with regularity, research suggests that their class ranking would improve by about 26 students.

Planning tactics include deciding in advance how, when, and where to study. Although one of the most important sets of skills for academic success, teachers often incorrectly assume students know them. Students should be instructed in planning when to study, setting study goals such as dividing up long assignments, and choosing suitable study environments. Further, teaching students to space their studying over time, rather than cramming at once, will increase their long-term retention.

Recording tactics include creating notes, diagrams, and illustrations from readings and lectures. Note taking is most effective when used to organize the connections between ideas, as opposed to summarizing or listing out individual key points. Note that summaries that are simple abridgments of content are ineffective, whereas summaries that are paraphrased abridgments tend to be more effective as they require deeper processing of the content. Providing exemplar notes for lectures have in some cases shown to make note taking more effective, although in general recording information is not as effective as retrieving it.

Text marking is the most popular and least effective category of study tactics. It includes activities such as highlighting, underlining, and circling words and passages. Text marking is popular because it is easy and creates the optics of learning, but in actuality, it is no more effective than just reading. Why is this the case? First, understanding a text requires connecting the ideas within it, rather than identifying and marking isolated items. Second, students need to understand a text before they are able to correctly identify the key ideas. In contrast to contributing to deeper understanding, text marking depends on it.

See also   Depth of Processing; Homework; Mnemonic Devices; Retrieval Practice

"Improving Students' Learning with Effective Learning Techniques: Promising Directions from Cognitive and Educational Psychology" by John Dunlosky et al., *Psychological Science in the Public Interest*, 2013, 14(1), 4–58; "Effects of Learning Skills Interventions on Student Learning: A Meta-Analysis" by John Hattie et al., *Review of Educational Research*, 1996, 66(2), 99–136.

DO ....

- ◆ Do teach students which study tactics work and which ones don't.
- ◆ Do ritualize retrieval practice in and out of class, offering frequent pre-tests, practice tests, quizzes, flashcards, active Q&A, and other activities requiring retrieval.
- ◆ Do assist students in planning the how, when, and where of studying, ensuring that they space their study sessions out over time.
- ◆ Do provide students exemplar notes that show how to connect ideas.
- ◆ Do encourage students to make and use their own tools for studying (e.g., flashcards).
- ◆ Do remind students: no effort, no learning.

 DON'T ....

- ◆ Don't let students waste time using study tactics that don't work.
- ◆ Don't promote highlighting, underlining, circling, or writing in the margins of books.
- ◆ Don't have students reread notes, lectures, or texts.
- ◆ Don't use summarization unless students receive training in proper summarization techniques (e.g., identifying and paraphrasing the most important ideas within a text).

REFLECT ....

Education generally focuses on what you study, such as algebra, the elements of the periodic table or how to conjugate verbs. But learning how to study can be just as important, with lifelong benefits. It can teach you to pick up knowledge faster and more efficiently and allow you to retain information for years rather than days.

—John Dunlosky

"What Works, What Doesn't" by John Dunlosky et al., *Scientific American Mind*, 2013, 24(4), 46–53.

48 Teach-to-Learn

The practice of teaching things to another person—real or hypothetical—for the purpose of improving the teacher's understanding.

There is no better way to learn about something than to have to explain or teach it to others. Whether the audience is real (e.g., a group of students) or hypothetical (e.g., "How would you explain this to a 5-year-old?"), the act of articulating explanations and teaching is a simple and effective instructional strategy. For example, take a middle-ranked student from a class of 100 students. When that student is required to teach instructional content to a peer—even role-playing teaching to an imaginary peer—research suggests their class ranking would improve by about 21 students.

The teach-to-learn method is similar to other oft-cited learning strategies, such as learning by teaching, elaborative interrogation, self-explanation, the platypus learning technique, and the Feynman Technique, but they all share the same basic operating mechanisms: First, when students explain something, they connect it to and activate prior knowledge, which grounds it more firmly in memory; second, students realize gaps in their understanding that they need to fill; third, by creating analogies and explaining what causes what, they perceive patterns and general principles across contexts; and fourth, by answering questions as explanations are presented, they are able to self-assess and practice retrieval from memory.

The greatest benefits occur when students are required to produce rich explanations versus explanations like "that's just how it works" or "that's what so-and-so said." By providing students with exemplars of quality explanations and teaching interactions, they are able to model their methods accordingly, using plain language versus jargon, highlighting connections between key elements, and drawing analogies to familiar concepts. Low-quality explanations do not benefit learning. The best explanations should span a range of topics and audiences. One way of doing this is through contrasting cases, which means, for example, explaining why one thing is true and why something different is false. Similarly, for advanced students, prompting them to teach to a variety of levels of audience introduces variation that can broaden their prior knowledge. In both of these approaches, students' increase their comprehension as well as their ability to transfer learning to new contexts.

While the time required for students to explain or teach everything they learn may be impractical, teaching them to employ this method on key concepts and skills will have the further benefit of developing productive learning habits, equipping students to become effective lifelong learners.

See also Depth of Processing; Peer Tutoring; Retrieval Practice; Study Tactics

---

"Eliciting Explanations: Constraints on When Self-Explanation Aids Learning" by Bethany Rittle-Johnson and Abbey Loehr *Psychonomic Bulletin & Review*, 2017, 24(5), 1501–1510; "Inducing Self-Explanation: A Meta-Analysis" by Kiran Bisra et al., *Education Psychology Review*, 2018, 1–23.

DO ···

- ◆ Do prompt students to explain what they are learning to others, real or hypothetical.
- ◆ Do model quality explanation and teaching.
- ◆ Do have students explain why incorrect things are incorrect and why correct things are correct.
- ◆ Do encourage the creation of novel metaphors, analogies, and examples as explanation techniques.
- ◆ Do vary the audience levels for the most advanced students.
- ◆ Do favor teach-to-learn in areas where there are common, overarching principles.
- ◆ Do combine teach-to-learn with contextual Q&A to promote retrieval practice.

 DON'T ···

- ◆ Don't interrupt explanations to correct them.
- ◆ Don't let students rely on notes or other resources when teaching or explaining.
- ◆ Don't use teach-to-learn on inessential concepts and information.

 REFLECT ···

Feynman Technique

Step 1: Identify a topic.
Step 2: Pretend teaching it to a child.
Step 3: Identify gaps in your understanding.
Step 4: Go to source material to fill gaps.
Step 5: Simplify explanations with stories and analogies.
Step 6: Go to Step 2.

—Richard Feynman

Attributed, see, for example, *Genius: The Life Science of Richard Feynman* by James Gleick, 1993, Vintage.

49 Technology-Based Instruction

The use of televisions, computers, tablets, or other devices to improve student learning.

Technology alone does not improve student learning—adding computers or tablets to K–12 classrooms will not, by itself, achieve anything beneficial, and can in many cases detract from learning experiences. Students learn just as well with or without technology as long as the content and methods of instruction are of high quality. Studies that compare the same high-quality instructional content and methods delivered with or without technology show no significant difference between modes of delivery. Contrary to Marshall McLuhan's famous aphorism, "The medium is the message," in learning contexts, the medium is not the message, the method is.

There is suggestive evidence that blending technology and direct instruction can produce better outcomes than instruction or technology-based learning alone. The question is how to achieve a favorable blend? Research suggests four areas where technology can be applied to simply and effectively complement traditional classroom instruction: creation, research, engagement, and data (CRED):

1. Creation—Using technology to enable students to create artifacts in support of their learning, both digital (e.g., videos, computer programs) and physical (e.g., 3D-printed objects), as opposed to only consuming technology.
2. Research—Using technology to access online resources that support research on topics of study, current events, and independent projects.
3. Engagement—Using technology to increase collaboration and classroom engagement (e.g., through the use of audience response systems).
4. Data—Using student data to better understand and address the learning needs of students (e.g., tracking and reporting student growth over the course of the year).

Technology-based solutions are often touted as an effective means of delivering differentiated instruction and accomplishing personalized learning. However, not only is the evidence supporting differentiated instruction and personalized learning weak to non-existent, it is weaker still when coupled with technology. Additionally, technology-based solutions come with significant administrative overhead. For example, lost or forgotten log-on credentials, failed Internet connections, buggy educational software, Nannyware restrictions, software updates, to name just a few, disrupt learning experiences, cut into instructional time, and often demotivate students. For this reason, professional development and just-in-time assistance are critical for technology-based instruction. For every dollar spent on technology, schools should budget a minimum of two dollars for curriculum design, training, and technology support.

See also Engagement, Student; Performance Load; Student-Directed Learning

---

"What Forty Years of Research Says about the Impact of Technology on Learning: A Second-Order Meta-Analysis and Validation Study" by Rana Tamim et al. *Review of Educational Research*, 2011, 81(1), 4–28; *The No Significant Difference Phenomenon* by Thomas Russell, 2001, IDECC; *The Feasibility of High-end Learning in a Diverse Middle School* by Catherine Brighton et al., September 2005, NRCG/T.

DO ··

- ◆ Do prioritize the quality of instruction and content over mode of delivery.
- ◆ Do favor a blended-technology approach over an all-direct-instruction or all-technology-based approach.
- ◆ Do use the CRED framework to guide the application of blended technologies.
- ◆ Do avoid technologies with significant administrative overhead and minimize existing administrative overhead wherever possible.
- ◆ Do support fellow teachers in the effective use of technology.
- ◆ Do engage in professional development in support of the effective use of technology.
- ◆ Do actively engage with students while they're using technology.

 DON'T ··

- ◆ Don't rely on technology alone to achieve student learning goals.
- ◆ Don't assume that computerized textbooks or workbooks will be more effective than their paper-based equivalents.
- ◆ Don't adopt the latest technology—i.e., the "latest shiny object"—thinking it will inspire more learning. It won't without the CRED framework.
- ◆ Don't underestimate the investment required to successfully deploy, use, support, and maintain technology-based instruction.

REFLECT ··

Information technologies are more like clothes than like fire. Fire is a wonderful technology because, without knowing anything about how it operates, you can get warm just standing close by. People sometimes find computers, televisions, and telecommunications frustrating because they expect these devices to radiate knowledge. But all information technologies are more like clothes; to get a benefit, you must make them a part of your personal space, tailored to your needs. New media complement existing approaches to widen our repertoire of communication; properly designed, they do not eliminate choices or force us into high tech, low touch situations.

—Christopher Dede

"Testimony to the House of Representatives Joint Hearing on Educational Technology in the 21st Century" by Christopher Dede, *Committee on Science and Committee on Economic and Educational Opportunities*, October 12, 1995.

50 Transfer

The application of prior learning to different contexts and domains.

Successful learning means that students can compute 2 + 2 in a classroom and then transfer that learning to adding coins to buy candy at the store. If this transfer doesn't occur, then in no meaningful way can it be said that arithmetic (or any other subject matter) has been learned. The problem is that this kind of transfer doesn't happen naturally. Our brains aren't wired for it. It can only reliably be achieved by design.

So what exactly is transfer and what can teachers do to improve it? There are two basic types of transfer: near and far. Near transfer occurs when prior learning can be applied to closely related contexts and performances, such as transferring adding coins in a classroom to adding coins in a store. Near transfer occurs easily and naturally, and this kind of apples-to-apples transfer is the type of skill transfer generally achieved in training contexts. Far transfer, by contrast, occurs when prior learning can be applied to very different contexts and performances, such as transferring the application of logic in computer programming to the application of logic in evaluating a political speech. Far transfer requires a kind of apples-to-oranges transfer, and it does not happen easily or naturally. And since the ultimate goal of education is to take what is learned in the classroom and apply it outside of the classroom, the proper question for teachers should be how to design learning experiences that promote far transfer?

There are three known ways to promote far transfer: (1) varying problem types, problem-solving methods, and learning contexts; (2) identifying deep structures and principles that can be generalized; and (3) using metaphors and analogies to bridge understanding.

Varying problem types, problem-solving methods, and learning contexts means having students solve problems of different types in different ways in different environments. The greater this mix, the greater the potential of transfer to new contexts. Identifying deep structures and principles means having students seek out patterns and heuristics that generalize. For example, understanding how the amplitude, frequency, and period of waves describe seemingly unrelated things like earthquakes, sound, gravity, and tsunamis. Using metaphors and analogies to bridge understanding means having students find similarities between things they know and things they don't, and then transferring related properties from the known to the unknown. For example, understanding the basic structure and dynamics of an atom by likening it to the solar system.

Research indicates that most classroom learning does not transfer outside of school. However, learning experiences designed to promote transfer can help students extend what they learn to everyday environments and realize the principal aim of education.

See also   Intelligence; Metacognition; Project-Based Learning; Teach-to-Learn

---

Education for Life and Work: Developing Transferable Knowledge and Skills in the 21st Century by National Research Council, 2013, National Academies Press; "Teaching for Transfer" by David Perkins and Gavriel Salomon, *Educational Leadership*, 1988, 46(1), 22–32.

✔ DO

- Do continually mix problem types, problem-solving methods, and learning contexts.
- Do favor students creating abstract representations of knowledge over highly contextualized representations.
- Do have students abstract general principles, patterns, and strategies from their work.
- Do have students regularly explore and practice analogies and metaphors.
- Do highlight the key features that allow a principle or strategy to be applied.

✘ DON'T

- Don't assume far transfer will happen.
- Don't confuse success on standardized tests with success transferring learning to real-world contexts.
- Don't vary learning contexts until students have basic proficiency.
- Don't overcontextualize initial learning experiences.
- Don't tell students the general principles, patterns, and strategies in advance.

❝ REFLECT

Transfer is a key concept in education and learning theory because most formal education aspires to transfer. Usually the context of learning (classrooms, exercise books, tests, simple streamlined tasks) differs markedly from the ultimate contexts of application (in the home, on the job, within complex tasks). Consequently, the ends of education are not achieved unless transfer occurs. Transfer is all the more important in that it cannot be taken for granted. Abundant evidence shows that very often the hoped-for transfer from learning experiences does not occur.

—David Perkins and Gavriel Salomon

"Transfer of Learning" by David Perkins and Gavriel Salomon, *International Encyclopedia of Education* (2nd ed.), Pergamon Press, 1994.

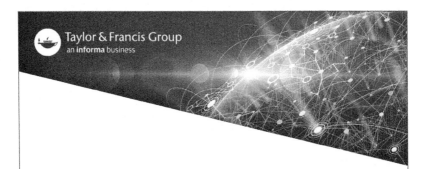

Made in the USA
Monee, IL
28 July 2021